Presidential
Libraries
and
Collections

Presidential Libraries and Collections

Fritz Veit

Greenwood Press

NEW YORK • WESTPORT, CONNECTICUT • LONDON

Library of Congress Cataloging-in-Publication Data

Veit, Fritz, 1907-
  Presidential libraries and collections.

  Bibliography: p.
  Includes index.
    1. Presidents—United States—Archives. I. Title.
CD3029.82.V45 1987   353.0085′2   86-25732
ISBN 0-313-24996-2 (lib. bdg. : alk. paper)

Library of Congress Catalog Card Number: 86-25732
ISBN: 0-313-24996-2

First published in 1987

Greenwood Press, Inc.
88 Post Road West, Westport, Connecticut 06881

Printed in the United States of America

The paper used in this book complies with the
Permanent Paper Standard issued by the National
Information Standards Organization (Z39.48-1984).

10 9 8 7 6 5 4 3 2 1

Contents

TABLES   ix

FIGURES   xi

PREFACE   xiii

INTRODUCTION   xv

1 Historical Overview   **1**

From Washington to Coolidge   1

From Hoover to the Present   5

Records of the Vice-President   15

2 Costs, and Measures to Reduce Them   **19**

Maintenance Costs of Presidential Libraries   19

Central Library or Individual Libraries?   21

Size Limitation of Buildings   23

Endowments and Other Gifts   25

Presidential Libraries Act of 1986   27

3 Archival Depository and Other Topics   31

What Constitutes an Archival Depository?   31

Nature of Presidential Papers   32

Liaison between White House and National Archives   34

Interpreting Data   35

Weeding   36

Computer Use   37

4 The Presidential Libraries Viewed as a Group   41

Holdings   41

Researcher Visits and Museum Visitors   42

Acquisition of Materials   46

Staffs of Presidential Libraries   49

Supporting Organizations   50

Instructions to Users   51

5 The Presidential Libraries: Individual
  Descriptions   57

Franklin D. Roosevelt Presidential Library   57

Harry S. Truman Presidential Library   63

Herbert Hoover Presidential Library   67

Dwight D. Eisenhower Presidential Library   70

John F. Kennedy Presidential Library   75

Lyndon B. Johnson Presidential Library   82

Nixon Presidential Materials Project   88

Gerald R. Ford Presidential Library and the Gerald
R. Ford Museum   93

Jimmy Carter Presidential Library   98

6 Papers of Presidents Preceding Hoover   **105**

Rutherford B. Hayes Library   115

John Adams and John Quincy Adams Papers   117

Millard Fillmore Papers   118

James Buchanan Papers   120

Warren G. Harding Papers   121

Additional Data for Several Collections   123

7 The Future   **129**

*Appendix 1: Cost of Presidential Libraries, FY 1955
through FY 1987*   *131*

Appendix 2: Presidential Libraries Questionnaire   *135*

*Appendix 3: Presidential Libraries' Supporting
Organizations*   *139*

BIBLIOGRAPHY   145

INDEX   149

Tables

1. Square Footage of the Presidential Libraries   24

2. Accessions and Holdings   42

3. Presidential Libraries Museum Visitors, 1947–1985   44

4. Presidential Libraries Researcher Visits, 1946–1985   45

5. Depositories and Purchases of Presidential Papers   107

6. Presidential Papers in the Library of Congress (Principal Accessions)   111

7. Microfilm Available for Papers Held by the Library of Congress   114

Figures

1. Categories of Materials   9
2. Cost of Operating and Maintaining Presidential Libraries   20
3. Presidential Libraries Museum Visitors, 1981–1985   47
4. Presidential Libraries Researcher Visits, 1981–1985   48

Preface

I am grateful to the many individuals who have supplied data. In particular I am indebted to James E. O'Neill, assistant archivist for presidential libraries, for generous advice and counsel and for materials prepared by his office.

I am also indebted to the directors of the presidential libraries and the presidential materials projects and to the directors of the other presidential materials collections for completing a questionnaire relating to their respective collections. Most directors sent literature pertaining to their collections, for which I thank them.

The directors or their representatives who furnished the data are listed below with the institutions they represent. Other respondents are recognized in the text where their answers to specific inquiries have been utilized.

William R. Emerson, director, Franklin D. Roosevelt Library.

Benedict M. Zabrist, director, Harry S. Truman library.

Robert Wood, director, Herbert Hoover Library.

John E. Wickman, director, Dwight D. Eisenhower Library.

William Johnson, chief archivist, John F. Kennedy Library.

Tina Lawson, supervisory archivist, Lyndon B. Johnson Library.

Ronald J. Plavchan, supervisory archivist, Nixon Presidential Materials Project.

Don W. Wilson, director, Gerald R. Ford Library and Museum.

William K. Jones, curator, Gerald R. Ford Museum.

Donald B. Schewe, director, Jimmy Carter Library.

Leslie H. Fishel, Jr., director, Rutherford B. Hayes Presidential Center.

John E. Cushing, librarian, Massachusetts Historical Society, and Celeste Walker, assistant editor, the Adams Papers.

Mary F. Bell, director of library and archives, Buffalo and Erie County Historical Society, Fillmore Papers.

Therese Snyder, the Historical Society of Pennsylvania, Buchanan Papers.

Gary J. Arnold, assistant archivist, Archives-Library Division, Ohio Historical Society, Harding Papers.

My thanks go also to Virginia McDavid, a colleague at Chicago State University, for reading the manuscript and for valuable editorial suggestions.

Introduction

This study is concerned with the collections of presidential papers from the beginning of U.S. history to the present. We shall see in the historical overview that the treatment of Presidential papers has been varied. With Raymond Geselbrecht, we may divide the history of presidential papers by distinct eras.[1]

The first era is characterized by treatment of presidential papers as private property and, as such, exclusively a president's concern. In the second era, it is recognized that a public interest exists in the papers. The public interest expressed itself in the acquisition by the federal government of certain presidential papers by gift and/or by purchase and in the protection and care of these papers by the Manuscript Division of the Library of Congress.

The ever-enlarging scope of the presidential office and the resulting sharp increase of presidential papers led to the third era.[2] The papers received by the Library of Congress up to the Roosevelt presidency amounted to 2 million pages; Franklin D. Roosevelt alone produced over 11 million pages. Even a person with Roosevelt's means could not provide a home and the necessary care for the papers and other materials he had gathered. Roosevelt was able to convince the lawmakers that it would be in the nation's interest to establish a federally supported archival depository. The Presidential Libraries Act of 1955 extended the privilege first granted to Roosevelt to future presidents and, under certain conditions, to earlier presidents, by offering them the possibility of forming depositories (libraries), which would be included in the presidential libraries system.

President Nixon's desire to control his papers completely, including the possibility of his destroying them at will, brought about a sharp negative reaction. It led to the Federal Records Act of 1978, which gave the government ownership, possession, and control of the presidential papers. The fourth era began with the enactment of this law.

I then describe the impact on Congress of the increasing cost of maintaining the presidential libraries. Congress considered a number of measures to reduce the outlay for the libraries. The result was the Presidential Libraries Act of 1986, which imposed mandatory endowments, a radical departure from hitherto voluntary contributions on the part of the president and the financial supporters of a presidential library.

Since mandatory endowments represent a basic change from the previous voluntary contributions on the part of the president and the private financial backers of a presidential library, it seems proper to add a fifth era to those suggested by Geselbrecht, an era marked by the Presidential Libraries Act of 1986.

I next present a number of topics selected for their continuing interest. They are combined in a chapter, but are independent of each other, and deal with such diverse subjects as the nature of presidential papers, "what constitutes an archival depository,?" weeding, and computer use in presidential libraries.

The two following chapters detail the libraries' holdings, their users, their staffs, their structures, and some details about the operation of the libraries. One chapter deals with the libraries as a group, the other with the libraries individually as separate entities. The descriptions and evaluations are based on many sources: questionnaire returns, information supplied by the Office of Presidential Libraries, government reports, and other pertinent literature. The questionnaires were sent out in late November and in early December 1984. (A sample copy appears as appendix 2.) This timing was probably responsible for the fact that the libraries did not report for identical time spans. Some responses covered 1984 and some 1985. Moreover, a few of the questions were not interpreted in a uniform fashion. For the sake of uniformity, I obtained data from the Office of Presidential Libraries for several of the categories that had already been covered by the questionnaires: holdings, researcher visits, museum visits, and budgets. For these categories, the figures used in text and tables are those supplied by the Office of Presidential Libraries.

The questionnaire replies of the libraries varied in completeness, details, and kind of information supplied, and these variations are reflected in the descriptions of the individual libraries.

The chapter concerned with the pre-Hoover collections is taken out of its historical sequence and follows the descriptions of the libraries in the presidential libraries system. By placing the chapter next to the evaluations of the libraries in the presidential libraries system, differences between the pre-Hoover collections and the presidential libraries can be readily discerned.

I have presented the six pre-Hoover collections for which the Library of Congress does not hold the bulk of the materials. Here, too, questionnaire replies were important sources of information. The questionnaires, which were submitted to the persons in charge of these collections, are similar to those addressed to the library directors in the presidential libraries system, although they omit items applicable only to libraries managed and supported by the federal government.

I hope that this study will facilitate the work of those who need to explore the vast amount of information concentrated in the presidential libraries and presidential papers collections. The study can serve the historians, the political scientists, journalists, legal scholars, librarians, and other researchers who wish to draw on the rich, and often unique, sources contained in the collections. Beyond this, members of the general public may wish to examine the study and be introduced to documents and memorabilia that may enlarge their understanding not only of the presidency but, more broadly, of the American political and social scene.

NOTES

1. Raymond Geselbrecht, "The Four Eras in the History of Presidential Papers." *Prologue* 15, no. 1 (Spring 1983): 37–42.

2. "Handling of Presidential Records: Historical and Current Practice," *in* U.S. Congress, House, Committee on Government Operations, *Presidential Records Act of 1978: Hearings on H.R. 10998 and Related Bills.* 95th Cong., 2d sess., appendix 10.

Presidential
Libraries
and
Collections

1

Historical Overview

FROM WASHINGTON TO COOLIDGE

Presidential libraries as we know them today are relatively new creations.[1] The Franklin D. Roosevelt Library, established in 1939 by joint resolution of Congress, was the first presidential library maintained by the federal government.[2] Earlier there had been an intermittent interest in preserving the papers of the presidents but no provision for housing the papers in a separate structure and providing for their care and utilization at the government's expense.

Presidential papers were considered private property. The presidents could dispose of them in any way they desired: keep them, give them away, sell them, or even destroy them. An examination of the papers created during the various presidencies shows that the papers differ from president to president in scope, quality, and quantity. "The most important factor in the creation of Presidential collections has been each President himself—his interests, his habits of conducting the business of his office, his concern with preserving a record of his administration. The comprehensiveness of a particular collection, as well as the character of its contents, depended upon the interests of a President as well as upon the events of his administration."[3]

George Washington recognized the importance of these papers not just for himself but also for the nation. He stated that they are a "species of public property, sacred in my hands."[4] Nevertheless, there was no doubt in his mind that they were his personal property and that he could grant or deny access to them at his pleasure. At the close of his presidency, Washington requested his secretaries to arrange and pack his papers for shipment to Mount Vernon, where he intended to erect at his own expense a building that would hold his military and civilian papers and could thus supply the data on which histories could be based.

Washington died in 1799 before his plan to build a structure to house his papers was carried out. After his death, his papers went by device to his nephew, Associate Justice of the Supreme Court Bushrod Washington, whose treatment of the papers was casual. He gave access to them freely. Supreme Court Justice John Marshall was permitted to consult the original papers while writing his life of George Washington. Jared Sparks, the editor of the *North American Review* who prepared a volume on the writings of George Washington, was invited to be Bushrod's house guest for three weeks. Not only was Sparks permitted to consult the materials while there, but he was also allowed to withdraw eight boxes of the papers and take them to Massachusetts. He carried the two containing the most important papers and shipped the remaining six. Jared Sparks kept the papers for ten years. After Bushrod Washington's death, the latter's nephew and heir, Corbin Washington, inherited them.

Although the theory and practice of treating the presidential papers as private property was not disputed, there evolved the view that a president's papers could be of considerable historical importance and deserved to be preserved. The State Department and later the Library of Congress supported these efforts. First, the State Department intermittently and then the Library of Congress more systematically gathered papers of former presidents, obtaining them as gifts or by purchase. Corbin Washington sold to the government George Washington's official records for $25,000 and, fifteen years later, the private papers for $20,000. The way the papers were treated by Washington and his heirs became the accepted way for all the other early presidents.

Until the end of the nineteenth century, a president had no choice but to remove the papers after the completion of his term of office, regardless of whether a suitable depository was available. Around the turn of the century, the Library of Congress Manuscript Division was created, which could serve as a depository for presidential papers. The presidents were not obligated to deposit their papers at the Library of Congress; however, at their discretion, they could avail themselves of this service. It is also significant that the president's office is established by the Constitution, not by statute. It does not have an institutional character like the various government departments—for instance, the State Department. The president's office was therefore not obligated, as were the government departments, to develop a procedure for a continuous institutional record. The handling of the presidential papers was to a large extent determined by the preferences of a president. Whatever the president wanted to handle himself, he kept in the White House; whatever he felt could be handled better by a department, he forwarded to the proper department for action. An example will illustrate the differences in treatment of the same set of circumstances by two presidents. During Washington's administration, applications for office were included in the Washington papers; the applications for office submitted during Polk's administration are in the Department of State files.[5] In Washington's case, they were treated as personal papers, in Polk's as public.

The papers created or received by the various presidents during their respective terms of office suffered very different fates.[6] Many of the presidents did not leave a full record, though they might have had the desire to preserve as complete files as possible. For instance, John Tyler designated his son and his two sons-in-law as his literary executors and bequeathed his papers to them. Because of the outbreak of the Civil War, some papers were removed to Richmond for safe quarters. There they were destroyed in the Richmond fire of April 2–3, 1865. The Tyler papers, which had been left in the Tyler home, were largely lost when the house was ransacked on various occasions by Union and Confederate soldiers. Similarly, many of Zachary Taylor's papers were lost during the Civil War. Many of William H. Harrison's papers were consumed by fire in peacetime when his log cabin burned down.

Papers of several presidents were destroyed intentionally, either by the presidents themselves or by their heirs. Chester A. Arthur, one day before his death in November 1886, asked his son to destroy the presidential papers. This request was not completely met. Chester A. Arthur III, President Arthur's grandson, on examining materials passed on to him, discovered papers from his grandfather's presidency.

Millard Fillmore collected all letters and documents received during his presidency, hoping that they would offer an authentic account of his administration. His son disregarded his father's wish and ordered that all papers be destroyed. Some papers survived anyway and may be found in the Buffalo Historical Society. Many of Abraham Lincoln's papers were destroyed by his son Robert Todd Lincoln. Most of the surviving Lincoln papers were acquired by the Library of Congress.

Benjamin Harrison hoped to make a collection "of the papers, manuscripts, autographs, badges, medals, and other such things belonging to me that might have public interest and to present it to a Historical Society where it might be kept safely and together instead of dividing them between my wife and children."[7] He was unable to carry out such an arrangement and had to leave the papers to his wife after all. They were not generally available, but several persons who considered writing a biography of Harrison were given access to them. The papers were taken to England by John L. Griffith, who served as U.S. consul, first in Liverpool and then in London. When he died suddenly in 1914, the president's widow succeeded in retrieving the papers from London.

Coolidge wanted most of his papers destroyed. Had not one of his assistants disregarded Coolidge's wish to destroy all personal files, practically no records of Coolidge's presidency would have survived. There were, however, presidents whose records were kept together from the outset and preserved. The Adams family was always conscious of the desirability, even the obligation, to preserve the accumulated records relating to the family. Similarly, William H. Taft and his family recognized the significance of his papers for an understanding of the social and political conditions of his time and took the necessary care to preserve them. Taft had an unusually wide range of important responsibilities and posts, occupying not only the office of president but also several other high offices.

The early presidents, without exception, held the view that the presidential papers were private property. Although challenged by some in the second half of the twentieth century, this position persisted until the Presidential Records Act of 1978 was passed.[8]

Pronouncements frequently cited in support of the view prevailing before the passing of the Presidential Records Act were made by Grover Cleveland and William Howard Taft. Cleveland said:

> I regard the papers and documents withheld and addressed to me or intended for my use and action purely unofficial and private, not infrequently confidential, and having reference to the performance of a duty exclusively mine. I consider them in no proper sense as . . . the

files of the Department, but as deposited there for my convenience, remaining still completely under my control.... [9]

Taft gave an accurate description of the views and the practices of his time:

> The Executive Office of the President is not a recording office. The vast amount of correspondence that goes through, signed either by the President or his Secretaries, does not become the property or a record of the government, unless it goes on to the official files of the department to which it may be addressed. The retiring President takes with him all of his correspondence, original and copies, which he carried on during his administration.... [10]

Most of the papers created during the presidencies extending from Washington to Coolidge were acquired by the Library of Congress by gift or purchase. The Library of Congress became the principal depository for the papers of twenty-three presidents, although several other depositories held the bulk of the papers of about a half-dozen presidents.

The collections of the pre-Hoover papers will be described in chapter 6, following the description and evaluation of the holdings of the libraries included in the presidential libraries system.

FROM HOOVER TO THE PRESENT

In the sequence of significant legislative developments dealing with presidential libraries, two landmarks stand out: the joint resolution of July 18, 1939, which established the Franklin D. Roosevelt Presidential Library, and the Presidential Libraries Act of 1955, which became law on August 12, 1955. The joint resolution applied specifically and only to the Roosevelt presidential library; the Presidential Libraries Act of 1955 allowed the federal government to accept any future presidential library without additional legislation.

The Presidential Libraries Act of 1955 authorizes the general services administrator to accept land, buildings, equipment, and gifts for the purpose of establishing a presidential archival depository and to operate it. He may accept papers and all kinds of other documents, objects, and materials that have a bearing on the career and life of the president as long as the materials have historical or commemorative value. A presidential library established in accordance with the Presidential Libraries Act of 1955 is more than a repository for presidential papers; it may include any kind of documents and objects that relate to the life and career of the president and generally to the political and social conditions prevailing during his life.

Beginning with Hoover, the presidents of the United States left the bulk of their presidential materials to the U.S. government, though they were not obligated to do so. The presidential materials have been deposited in presidential libraries and thus became available to the public at large. This tradition was broken by President Richard Nixon. He was not prepared to continue this practice. On September 7, 1974, nearly a month after he resigned from office, Richard Nixon concluded an agreement with Arthur F. Sampson, the Administrator of the General Services Administration, which provided for a very different disposition of presidential materials.[11] The agreement stipulates that until such time as a permanent archival depository is established to house the Nixon presidential materials, the materials would be moved to a temporary depository located in California near Nixon's home. Access to the materials could be gained only by the use of two keys—one kept by Mr. Nixon and the other by the archivist or his representative. The agreement stipulated further that for a three-year period, only copies of the deposited materials could be produced and withdrawn. If persons other than the former President wished to have copies, they would have to obtain Mr. Nixon's written permission. After the lapse of three years, the President could withdraw any or all materials from deposit and retain such withdrawn materials for any use he might wish to make of them—even destroy them. The tape recordings would remain on deposit until September 1, 1979. Then they would be donated to the United States under the condition that they be destroyed on September 1, 1984, or on Richard Nixon's death, should death occur earlier.

Many members of Congress and most of the scholarly world reacted adversely to the Nixon-Sampson agreement. The sentiment against the provisions of the agreement was so strong that Congress passed legislation to preserve the presidential papers and other materials and to facilitate their accessibility. The law providing for the protection and preservation of the Nixon tapes and other presidential historical materials was passed on December 19, 1974, referred to as the Presidential Recordings and Materials Preservation Act.[12] Title I of the act deals exclusively with the Nixon presidential materials.

Although the projected destruction of the Nixon tapes was the impetus for this legislation, it was felt that the whole issue of the ownership, preservation, and accessibility of presidential materials should be fully explored and resolved. Title I of the act was therefore supplemented by title II, which stipulated that a study commission should be established. A major task of the commission, the National Study Commission on Records and Documents of Federal Officials, was to consider "whether the historical practice regarding the records produced by and on behalf of the Presidents of the United States should be rejected or accepted."[13] The commission completed a final report and an alternate report on March 31, 1977.[14] These reports became important sources for subsequent hearings dealing with the Freedom of Information Act and, generally, for legislation to ensure public access to the official historically significant papers of the presidents.

The purpose of title I of the act is to safeguard and protect the Nixon presidential materials.[15] To attain this objective, the administrator of the general services administration (administrator) was required to take possession of the Nixon tape recordings, papers, documents, memorandums, transcripts, and other objects that constitute historical presidential materials. The law prescribed that title I of the act be implemented by regulations.[16] The regulations, accompanied by a report, were to be submitted by the administrator to both Houses of Congress within ninety days of enactment of the law.

Since both Houses considered the fate of the Nixon tapes and of the other Nixon presidential materials of utmost importance, both the Senate and the House held hearings on the regulations.[17] The regulations as submitted by the administrator underwent four drafts before they were approved by Congress. With two exceptions, the changes were largely technical in nature.[18]

In developing the regulations, the administrator had to consider seven criteria:[19]

1. As early as feasible, the public has to be provided with the full truth of the abuses of governmental power, abuses generally identified with the term *Watergate*.

2. Recordings and materials are to be made available in judicial proceedings.

3. General access to information relating to the nation's security can be allowed only in accordance with appropriate judicial procedures.

4. Every individual's right to a fair and impartial trial must be protected.

5. Any party must have the opportunity to assert any legally or constitutionally based right to prohibit or limit access to the recordings and other materials.

6. The public must be provided access to historically significant materials unless these materials are required in the Watergate proceedings.

7. Richard Nixon or his heirs must be given sole custody and use of materials that are not related to the need stated in criterion 1 and are not otherwise of general historical significance.

Figure 1 shows the categories covered by the act, as well as those not covered.[20] Not subject to the act are prepresidential materials, private or personal items, nonpresidential materials, such as federal records, and nonhistorical materials.

In both the House and the Senate hearings, concern was shown about the need to treat Mr. Nixon fairly. The chairman of the Senate committee, Senator Abraham Ribicoff, in particular considered this an important factor. He said: "We must treat Mr. Nixon just as fairly as we would any subsequent President. This is what concerns me, and I feel that it concerns the Committee also."[21]

The regulations reflect the criteria set down in title I of the act. They impose restrictions on the use of certain categories of materials, taking into account the practices of former presidents, as well as the needs and the sometimes conflicting interests as outlined in the act.[22] Restricted are materials that might represent a clearly un-wanted invasion of personal privacy, constitute a libel of a living person, or compromise national security.[23]

In order to make Watergate-related materials available as quickly and as extensively as possible and in order to obtain the truth in contested interpretations, fewer restrictions were imposed on Wa-tergate-related materials than on other materials.

In accordance with the law, the regulations provided that mate-rials in the custody of the government that were private or personal or not of general historical relevance were to be returned to the president.

Prior to opening materials for public access, the administrator must assign archivists to do the initial processing. The boxes must be shelved in alphabetical, numerical, or other sequence; a location register and cross-index of the boxes must be established; and finding aids must be produced. Materials must be reviewed so that those that may be subject to restrictions can be identified, items in poor physical condition can be discovered and their preservation ensured, and tape recordings can be reproduced and transcribed.[24]

If complete files cannot be released, portions representing integral file segments may be released. "The term [integral file segment] refers to a portion of processed materials, having a logical integrity, whose opening to the public, as determined by the processing ar-chivist, will not impede the processing, including the arrangement and preparation of finding aids, of other segments of the materials."[25]

In contrast to former presidents, Richard Nixon does not have

Figure 1
Categories of Materials

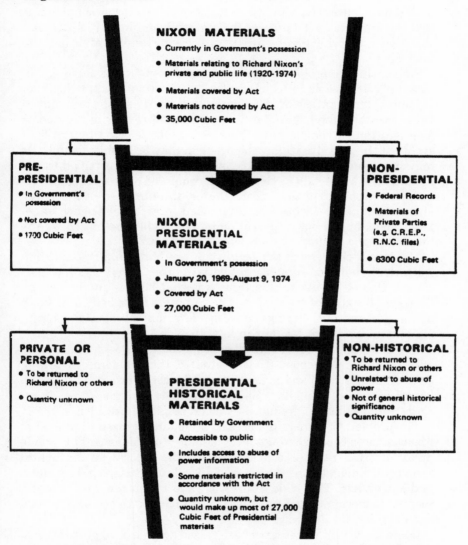

NIXON MATERIALS
- Currently in Government's possession
- Materials relating to Richard Nixon's private and public life (1920-1974)
- Materials covered by Act
- Materials not covered by Act
- 35,000 Cubic Feet

PRE-PRESIDENTIAL
- In Government's possession
- Not covered by Act
- 1700 Cubic Feet

NON-PRESIDENTIAL
- Federal Records
- Materials of Private Parties (e.g. C.R.E.P., R.N.C. files)
- 6300 Cubic Feet

NIXON PRESIDENTIAL MATERIALS
- In Government's possession
- January 20, 1969-August 9, 1974
- Covered by Act
- 27,000 Cubic Feet

PRIVATE OR PERSONAL
- To be returned to Richard Nixon or others
- Quantity unknown

NON-HISTORICAL
- To be returned to Richard Nixon or others
- Unrelated to abuse of power
- Not of general historical significance
- Quantity unknown

PRESIDENTIAL HISTORICAL MATERIALS
- Retained by Government
- Accessible to public
- Includes access to abuse of power information
- Some materials restricted in accordance with the Act
- Quantity unknown, but would make up most of 27,000 Cubic Feet of Presidential materials

Source: Report to Congress on Title I Presidential Recordings and Materials Preservation Act, *In* U.S. Congress, Senate, Committee on Government Operations, *GSA Regulations Implementing Presidential Recordings and Materials Preservation Act. Hearing*, 94th Cong., 1st sess., 1975, p. 95.

custody of his presidential historical materials; therefore it is not he but the federal government, acting through the archivist, that restricts and releases materials and that ensures the protection of individual rights. The administrator, Arthur Sampson, emphasizes that the archivists who process the materials are highly skilled and objective and take great care in processing and evaluating the materials.[26]

Since complex problems may arise, the regulations have established review panels to which difficult determinations, or those requiring interpretation of the regulations, or those of precedential value may be submitted. The first instance of review is the Senior Archival Panel, composed of three archivists selected by the U.S. archivist. In rare situations, the problem may be highly complex or may involve a major precedent. Such cases may be certified to the Presidential Materials Review Board, composed of these three members: the archivist of the United States, the librarian of Congress, and a third person, who is distinguished in archival science or related fields but is not a federal employee, to be nominated by the Council of the Society of American Archivists.[27]

Mr. Nixon challenged the legality of the Materials Preservation Act, which deprived him of prerogatives other presidents had possessed. One of his major objections was that he was singled out by Congress for special treatment. The Supreme Court ruled in favor of the government, taking into consideration the special circumstances under which Mr. Nixon left office.[28]

The National Study Commission prepared reports—a final report and an alternate report—that evaluated the problems regarding control, disposition, and preservation of records produced by or on behalf of federal officials.[29] Special consideration was given to records and documents produced by or on behalf of presidents.

The problem of ownership, preservation, and accessibility of presidential records occupied not only members of Congress but a wide array of other persons concerned with the federal governmental structure, among them historians, political scientists, legal scholars, and journalists. This wide interest is reflected in the letters, statements, memoranda, and court decisions included in the hearings on the Presidential Records Act.

Some important voices have been raised against a suggested transfer of presidential papers to governmental ownership at the conclusion of a presidential term. The opponents of change of the nearly 200-year-old practice felt that the presidents and their close advisers might not commit to paper many thoughts if all papers relevant to public business would be considered official records and as such be exposed to public scrutiny soon after a president finished his term of office. John S. D. Eisenhower, President Dwight D. Eisenhower's son and assistant in military and civilian life, suggested that "the quality of advice a President would receive in office would certainly degenerate, or be unrecorded if advisers spoke for 'the record,' conscious that their words would be made public at the end of a President's term."[30] The overwhelming majority of the statements and comments, however, were in favor of treating the papers as public property. Representative John Brademas expressed the conviction of the majority when he emphasized that it makes no sense any longer to consider as property of one individual the work produced by literally thousands of government employees hired with taxpayers' money.[31] Following past practice, the majority decided to impose a number of restrictions to prohibit the immediate disclosure of certain categories of presidential papers. Representative Brademas gave these reasons for the restrictions: "Once again, we felt that the threat of immediate disclosure of Presidential materials upon the end of a President's term of office could well have a chilling effect on the willingness of his staff to express potentially controversial views—a process vital to the President for the proper conduct of his office."[32] Seventeen of the nineteen members of the Public Documents Committee therefore favored a buffer period to ensure that the president and his advisers could set down their ideas in writing without fear of premature disclosure.[33]

The result of extensive deliberations and hearing of witnesses was the Presidential Records Act, passed on November 4, 1978.[34] It contains these main features:

1. It establishes public ownership of presidential records, defined as records created by future presidents and their staff in the course of discharging their public duties. (As a preliminary, the act defines the terms *presidential records*, *personal records*, and *documentary material* as used in the act.)

2. It establishes procedures governing the preservation of the records and specifies the conditions of their public availability after the presidents have ended their term of office.

3. It establishes the effective date with respect to public ownership of presidential records: the term of office of the president beginning on or after January 21, 1981. Since article I, section 2, of the Constitution prescribes that the president shall hold office during a term of four years, the individual who takes the oath of office on January 20, 1981, "is deemed to take office on this date, regardless of his previous service in that office."[35] Ronald Reagan is the first president to whom the act applies.

Presidential records are defined as records created or received by the president in performance of his official duties. This definition is broad. It includes all records except agency records subject to the Freedom of Information Act and personal records.[36]

Personal records are the materials that are neither developed in connection with nor utilized in the transaction of government business.[37] The scope of the term *personal records* is narrow. Some activities that one would generally consider private and personal would be treated as presidential since they may have an impact on the conduct of presidential affairs. If, for instance, a family member such as a president's wife, son, or daughter serves as a de facto member of the president's staff, the documents reflecting this type of service would be considered presidential. Further, many political activities affect his official duties. Such political activities would therefore not be considered personal, and records documenting the activities would be treated as presidential.[38]

The law stipulates that the records become government property and must be transferred to the custody of the U.S. archivist immediately upon the conclusion of a presidential term. The archivist has the choice of placing them in a presidential library or in another federally operated facility.[39]

The law follows past practice in permitting a president to impose restrictions with regard to certain categories of papers.[40] The exemptions are modeled after the restrictions contained in the Freedom of Information Act. It is, however, important to distinguish between the mandatory restrictions imposed by the president and the restrictions imposed in accordance with the Freedom of Information Act. The statutorily permitted restrictions imposed by the president are binding and must be observed. The restrictions imposed in accordance with the Freedom of Information Act are discretionary.

There are six categories of information to which access may be restricted by the president:

1. Information authorized to be kept secret by an executive in the interest of national defense or foreign policy.

2. Information relating to presidential appointments.

3. Material exempted from disclosure by another statute.

4. Trade secrets and confidential business information.

5. Confidential communications between the president and his advisers.

6. Information whose disclosure would result in an unwarranted invasion of personal privacy.

Nine categories are exempted from disclosure by the Freedom of Information Act:[41]

1. Classified foreign policy and defense material.
2. Records relating solely to an agency's internal personnel rules and practices.
3. Documents specifically exempted from dislosure by statute.
4. Privileged and confidential trade secrets and data.
5. Interagency files.
6. Personal and medical files.
7. Law enforcement investigatory files that would not be available to a person in litigation with an agency.
8. Certain information relating to financial institutions.
9. Geological and geophysical information.

For categories 1, 3, 4, and 6 of the president-imposed mandatory exemptions, there are comparable exemptions under the Freedom of Information Act. There are no comparable exemptions under the Freedom of Information Act to the president-imposed mandatory exemptions of categories 2 and 5.

The six categories listed as subject to mandatory exemptions are the only categories of records to which the president may restrict access. He does not have the authority to impose additional restrictions on records of his administration. The president is given several options. He may restrict access to all six categories; he may restrict access to only some of the six categories; and he may restrict access to a selected group of documents within any of the six categories. Further, he may impose the restriction for any category or a specific item within a category either for the maximum period of twelve years or for a shorter period.

The mandatory restrictions must be imposed by the president while he is still in office. This prerogative may not be delegated to the archivist or any other person to be carried out after the president has left office or died.[42] The availability of records not subject to mandatory presidential restrictions is governed by the Freedom of Information Act. Also subject to the Freedom of Information Act are documents whose mandatory restrictions have expired after twelve years, or earlier if the president has removed the restrictions earlier, or if the materials have come into public domain by their publication by the president or his White House associates.

A document, either the original or a copy found both in the presidential library and in the files of a federal agency, can be released by the agency under the Freedom of Information Act.[43]

Even if materials are not restricted, a user may not be able to obtain them immediately. Time is required for processing; the archivist has five years to complete this task.[44]

If the archivist has determined that an item is subject to a president-imposed mandatory restriction, such determination is not subject to judicial review. A would-be user may, however, make an administrative appeal, which would ensure a written determination by the archivist within thirty days as to whether the access to the record was properly denied.

The materials that are mandatorily restricted and therefore not available to the general public are available to the incumbent president and to Congress if the materials are not otherwise available and are required for the conduct of official business. The materials also remain available to the former president and his designated representatives.[45]

To ensure a reliable and complete record, the president is advised and encouraged to follow sound management practices and to document the performance of his functions as fully as possible.[46] The extent to which the president carries out these requirements depends largely on his judgment and on the degree of his cooperation. The president is also required to separate personal papers from presidential papers.[47] This should prove to be a minor task inasmuch as few records are exclusively personal in character.

If, while in office, the president wishes to dispose of materials that he believes have no historical, administrative, informational, or evidentiary value, he must first obtain the written views of the archivist. Sixty legislative days before taking action, the president must submit to Congress the disposal schedule accompanied by the archivist's written view. Once the disposal schedule has been established, it remains operative for future disposals of the same kind of materials, unless amended.[48]

After the presidential records have been turned over to the U.S. archivist and are under his custody, he may dispose of records that in his judgment have no historical, administrative, informational, or evidentiary value. He must publish a notice in the *Congressional Record* of his intent to dispose of such records sixty legislative days before taking action. The sixty-day period allows public inspection of the materials intended for disposal and can lead to enjoining the proposed action.[49]

In the personnel area, the archivist has the prerogative of appointing the director of the presidential library. The archivist must consult with the president in whose administration the library records have been created or received. Although it may be assumed that the former president's preference will be given great weight, he does not have the right to veto the appointment.[50]

RECORDS OF THE VICE-PRESIDENT

The vice-president has the same authority and responsibility regarding the vice-presidential records as has the president regarding his presidential records. The archivist applies the same rules to vice-presidential materials as he does to presidential materials.

There are a number of choices in handling vice-presidential documents. Should a vice-president later become president, he would most likely wish to deposit his vice-presidential materials with the records of his presidency. If he does not become president, he may deposit his records with those of the president under whom he served, or he may place them in another federal depository or in a nonfederal depository if the archivist deems this to be in the public interest. This flexibility does not include the option of establishing a separate library for vice-presidential records.[51]

The historic overview would not be complete without reference to an important change that occurred on May 17, 1986, when the president approved Public Law 99–323. This act, designed to reduce the cost of operating presidential libraries, may be cited as the Presidential Libraries Act of 1986. It imposes mandatory endowments. For a detailed presentation of the problem of cost reduction and of the endowment provisions in particular, see Chapter 2.

NOTES

1. The main source for the following discussion is "Handling of Presidential Records: Historical and Current Practice," *in* U.S. Congress, House, Committee on Government Operations, *Presidential Records Act of 1978: Hearings on H.R. 10998 and Related Bills*, 95th Cong., 2d sess., 1978, appendix 10, pp. 467–529 (hereafter cited as appendix 10).

2. See chapter 5 for details regarding the establishment, status, and scope of the Franklin D. Roosevelt Library.

3. Appendix 10, p. 467.

4. Ibid., p. 473.

5. Ibid., p. 478.

6. Ibid., pp. 480–83.

7. Herbert R. Collins and David B. Weaver, eds., *Wills of the U.S. Presidents* (New York: Communication Channels, 1976), p. 151. Also quoted in appendix 10, pp. 478–79.

8. Public Law, 95–591; 92 Stat. 2523; 44 USC 101, n. 2107, 2108, 2201–07.

9. James D. Richardson, ed., *A Compilation of the Messages and Papers of the Presidents* (New York: Bureau of National Literature, 1897), 10: 4963. Also quoted in appendix 10, p. 483.

10. William Howard Taft, *Our Chief Magistrate and His Powers* (New York: Columbia University Press, 1916), p. 34. Also quoted in appendix 10, pp. 486–87.

11. "Nixon-Sampson Agreement Relating to Presidential Materials," *in* U.S. Congress, House, Committee on House Administration, *The "Public Documents Act": Hearings on H.R. 16902 and Related Legislation*, 93d Cong. 2d sess., 1974, pp. 235–37. Dated September 6, 1974, and accepted by Arthur Sampson September 7.

12. Public law 93–526, 88 Stat. 1695–1702.

13. Public law 93:526, sec. 201, 3317 (1), 88 Stat. 1699.

14. U.S. Congress, House, Committee on Government Operations, *Presidential Records Act of 1978, Hearings on H.R. 10998 and Related Bills*, 95th Cong., 2d sess., 1978, appendix 8, Final Report of the National Study Commission on Records and Documents of Federal Officials, March 31, 1977, pp. 433–47; Appendix 9: Alternate Report of Minority Members of National Study Commission on Records and Documents of Federal Officials, March 31, 1977, pp. 448–66.

15. Public law 93–526, sec. 101–106, Title I: Preservation of Presidential Recordings and Materials.

16. Ibid., sec. 103–4.

17. U.S. Congress, House, Commmittee on House Administration, *GSA Regulations to Implement Title I of the Presidential Recordings and Materials Preservation Act: Hearings on S. 4016*, 94th Cong., 1st sess., 1975; U.S. Congress, Senate, Committee on Government Operations, *GSA Regulations Implementing Presidential Recordings and Materials Preservation Act: Hearing*, 94th Cong., 1st sess., 1975; Report to Congress on Title I: Presidential Recordings and Materials Preservation Act, dated March 1975, appears in the *Senate Hearing*, pp. 79–286.

18. For a detailed account, see Arnold Hirshon, "Recent Developments in the Accessibility of Presidential Papers and Other Presidential Historical Materials," *Government Publications Review* 6, no. 4 (1974): 348–52.

19. Public law 93–526, sec. 104.

20. *Senate Hearing on GSA Regulations*, p. 95.

21. Ibid., p. 8.

22. See especially Arthur Sampson's testimony in Ibid., pp. 11–14.

23. The original draft of the regulations gave a broader protection by imposing restrictions on the accessibility of materials that would tend to embarrass, damage, or harass living persons. See Hirshon, "Recent Developments," p. 350.

24. *Senate Hearing on GSA Regulations*, pp. 165–66.

25. Ibid., p. 171.

26. Ibid., p. 13.

27. Ibid., pp. 180–85.

28. Hirshon, "Recent Developments," pp. 346–52.

29. See note 14 for full title of reports.

30. John S. D. Eisenhower, "Those Presidential Papers," *New York Times*, January 12, 1975 (reprinted in *Senate Hearing on GSA Regulations*, pp. 240–42). See also Arthur Schlesinger, Jr., "Who Owns a President's Papers?" *Wall Street Journal*, February 26, 1975 (reprinted in *Senate Hearing on GSA Regulations*, pp. 234–39); Alexandra K. and David Wigdor, "The Future of Presidential Papers," in Harold C. Relyea et al., *The Presidency and Information Policy* (New York: Center for the Study of the Presidency, Proceedings 4, no. 1 (1981), pp. 92–101; Herman Kahn, "The Presidential Library: A New Institution," *Special Libraries* 50, no. 3 (March 1959): 106–7.

31. *Hearings on Presidential Records Act of 1978* (1978), p. 72.

32. Ibid.

33. Ibid.

34. Public law 95–591, 92 Stat. 2523.

35. U.S. Congress, House, Committee on Government Operations, *Presidential Records Act of 1978. Report to Accompany H.R. 13500*, 95th Cong., 2d sess, 1978, H. Rept. 95–1487, pt. I, p. 18.

36. Ibid., pp. 3, 11–12, 4; USC 2201(2).

37. Ibid., 44 USC 2201(3).

38. Ibid.

39. Ibid.

40. Ibid., pp. 3–4, 14–17, 44 USC 2204.

41. 5 USC 552(b).

42. H. Rept. 95–1487, pt. I, p. 17, 44 USC 2204(d).

43. *Hearings on Presidential Records Act of 1978* (1978), pp. 156–57.

44. H. Rept. 95–1487, pt. I, p. 4, 16, 44 USC 2204(b)(2).

45. Ibid., p. 17, 44 USC 2205(3).

46. Ibid., p. 23, 44 USC 2203(a).

47. Ibid., p. 12, 44 USC 2203(b).

48. Ibid., p. 13, 44 USC 2203(c).

49. Ibid., p. 13, 44 USC 2203(d)(3).

50. Ibid., p. 13, 44 USC 2203(d)(2).

51. Ibid., p. 18, 44 USC 2207.

2

Costs, and Measures to Reduce Them

MAINTENANCE COSTS OF PRESIDENTIAL LIBRARIES

Expenditures for the maintenance of presidential libraries have grown through the years much more rapidly than anticipated and to levels not envisaged when the Presidential Libraries Act was passed in 1955. The first year, it cost $63,745 to maintain a presidential library. At that time, it was estimated that at the end of one hundred years, there would be twelve to fifteen presidential libraries, whose maintenance would amount to $1.5 million per year.[1] This estimate proved to be way off the mark. Within less than thirty years, there were seven libraries, costing about $14 million a year to maintain.[2] (See figure 2.)

The annual expenditures from 1955 to 1985 for each library and each presidential materials project are recorded in appendix 1. Although there are occasional decreases in annual expenditures, the

Figure 2
Cost of Operating and Maintaining Presidential Libraries

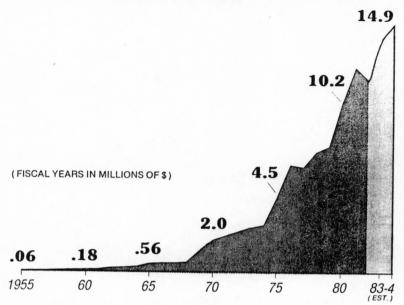

(FISCAL YEARS IN MILLIONS OF $)

.06   .18   .56   2.0   4.5   10.2   14.9

1955   60   65   70   75   80   83-4
(EST.)

Source: U.S. Congress, Senate, Committee on Governmental Affairs, *Former Presidents Facilities and Reform Act of 1983: Report together with Minority Views to Accompany S. 563*, 98th Cong., 2d sess., 1984, S. Rept. 98–637, p. 26.

general trend toward increases is clearly evident. Beginning in fiscal year 1982, the administrator released the presidential libraries from payment of SLUC (standard level user charges) to the Federal Buildings Fund. From 1982 on, the fund was reimbursed only on the basis of actual costs. One may therefore wonder why the charges in the SLUC and actual cost column in the appendix table increased after 1982. These increases are explained in a letter to the author:

> In 1981, we added a temporary storage facility in Atlanta for the Carter Presidential materials; 1982 was the first full year that this facility was in operation.
>
> Also in 1981, we added the Ford Library and Museum to our Presidential Libraries system; 1982 was the first full year that these two facilities were in operation.
>
> Extensive repair and alteration projects—neglected by the General Services Administration in the years preceding 1982—have had to be undertaken since that time at the Libraries. These have included the construction of a new roof at the Truman Library; the repair of the sea wall and the installation of a new heating and air conditioning

system at the Kennedy Library; and the improvement of fire and other safety measures at the Johnson Library.[3]

Members of Congress have become apprehensive of these continuous increases in cost and have sought ways and means to halt the increases and, if possible, to reverse the trend. This movement is reflected in bills introduced in recent Congresses and in corresponding hearings and reports.[4] These documents suggest various methods. The main questions are concerned with these topics:

1. Should there be a separate library for each president or a central library?
2. Who should defray the cost of maintaining presidential libraries: the private sector or the government, or both?
3. Should the role of endowments be enlarged?

Congress attained one of its goals by passing H.R. 1349 - 99th Cong. in spite of reservations expressed by leading archival officials about several of the key provisions of the bill. The bill, which became public law 99–323, and was named the Presidential Libraries Act of 1986, will be discussed at the end of this chapter.

From the beginning, the establishment and support of Presidential libraries has been considered a joint public-private sector effort. Following the pattern established by the Roosevelt Library, all the presidential libraries subsequently formed have left to private initiative to seek and collect funds for building the library. In all these instances, the former presidents have been able to choose the locality and, aided by their supporters, also decide on the size and design of the building. With the exception of the Lyndon B. Johnson Library and the Gerald R. Ford Library, the general services administrator has obtained title to the presidential library buildings. The University of Texas has retained title to the building in which the Lyndon B. Johnson Library is housed; similarly, the University of Michigan has retained title to the building housing the Ford Library. Yet regardless of who holds the title, the buildings are maintained and operated by the federal government.

CENTRAL LIBRARY OR INDIVIDUAL LIBRARIES?

In its search for economies, Congress has explored repeatedly the possibility of creating a central library in Washington in lieu of establishing a separate library for each president. The merits of this alternative were discussed by Congress as early as 1955 in the course of the hearings dealing with the Presidential Libraries Act.[5] In these early discussions, the individual presidential library emerged as the accepted pattern.

Recent hearings on bills designed to reduce expenditures for presidential libraries have again dealt extensively with the question of whether a central presidential library would result in economies and other advantages over an individual library for each president. The statements by William J. Anderson, Ray Kline, and Robert M. Warner submitted in the course of hearings are particularly helpful in clarifying the arguments for and against a central presidential library.[6]

A complete central library would bring together the materials of all presidents now maintained under the Presidential Libraries Act in separate libraries, as well as the materials that would be produced in future presidencies. Realistically this would seem impossible. Not only would it be prohibitively expensive to move all materials held by the several presidential libraries to Washington, but there would not be sufficient professional and citizen support for depriving communities now seats of presidential libraries of one of their cherished cultural and educational assets. Legal objections could also be raised since each of the several presidents or his heirs made the donations of materials with the understanding that they would be housed in a separate building at a specific location.

A central library could be considered only for future presidential materials collections. It would have to be a partial central library beside which the several libraries spanning the presidencies from Hoover to Reagan would continue to exist and be maintained. A central presidential library, even a partial central library, would have certain advantages. Researchers interested in the activities of more than one president could satisfy their research needs at one place and would not have to travel to several locations, perhaps thousands of miles apart.

A central library would offer certain economies. Space devoted to specific uses such as common support areas could be optimized, and staffing levels might be lower than in dispersed individual libraries.[7] But a central library, even with the limited scope of covering only future presidencies, has negative features that vastly outweigh its advantages. If concentrated at one location in Washington, a library would be more vulnerable to loss, especially in case of war. Materials are safer when dispersed.

Further, space needs would have to be anticipated. This cannot be done with any degree of certainty beyond any one president's term. Another element is the possible impact of automation. Although the rate of growth has been accelerating with each president, this need not be the case in the future since automation and miniaturization may reduce future space requirements.

In favor of continuing the provision of an individual library for each president, additional points may be noted. All presidential libraries have been built with private funds. Therefore the government does not have to bear construction costs. The location, design, and size of the buildings have been largely determined by the presidents and their associates and supporters. The libraries have been placed in regions where the presidents had their roots. Presidential materials can be made available to a larger group of people than if all materials were contained in one large building. The libraries provide unique cultural resources, some of particular regional significance.

The museum aspect of the presidential libraries can be given due consideration. In a central library it might have to be severely curtailed or even eliminated.

Presidents would be more inclined to donate materials to a library devoted to their presidency alone than to a center containing papers and other materials from several presidents. It should be emphasized that the Presidential Records Act requires only that presidential records become public property at the close of a president's term of office. Presidents retain personal records and can dispose of them as they wish. It may be assumed that presidents would be inclined to turn all or most of these over to a library bearing their name, while they probably would not donate personal records to a central library where the records would lose their prominence and uniqueness.

SIZE LIMITATION OF BUILDINGS

Members of Congress have considered ways of reducing the costs of individual library buildings. To this end, several bills have been introduced that would rigidly limit the size of new presidential library structures. For instance, Senate bill 563 introduced in the Ninety-eighth Congress required that a library facility not exceed 60,000 square feet if the president has not served more than a term of four years. If the president, or former vice-president, has served more than a term of four years, then the facility should not exceed more than 70,000 square feet. These figures include space for museum purposes.

A subsequent committee report, House report 99–125, did not recommend adoption of the space limitations provisions of the bills.[8] In accordance with the view expressed by the U.S. archivist, the committee acknowledged that the appropriate size of a building has

Table 1
Square Footage of the Presidential Libraries

Library	Gross Sq. Footage	Storage, Archival & Museum	Area for Review, incl. Public Ref. & Staff Work Rms.	Museum Display
Hoover	30,000	8,397	4,380	6,530
Roosevelt	51,000	16,576	3,823	9,739
Truman	96,000	8,201	11,199	14,108
Eisenhower	88,000	18,013	6,346	22,145
Kennedy	95,000	13,729	9,846	15,980
Johnson	117,000	37,140	12,690	22,272
Ford	78,000	15,216	8,996	18,246

2.   How are the 70,000 sq. ft. of the Carter library to be divided between space for storage of Presidential records, areas for review of those records, and museum displays?

Carter	70,000	19,818	3,430	15,269

Source: U.S. Congress, House, Committee on Government Operations, *Presidential Libraries Funding: Hearing on H.R. 3138 and Related Bills*, 98th Cong., 2d sess., 1984, p. 153.

to depend on many factors, in particular the length and scope of a president's career, donations of materials by the president's associates, processing of materials, the possibility of miniaturization and automation, and expected use. If due consideration is given to these factors, standards or guidelines can be developed that are flexible and ensure efficient space use. That efficiency of space use has not always been considered essential is evident from past practices. The Hoover Library is the most efficient, with 71 percent of its gross footage devoted to usable space. The Kennedy Library, at the other end of the scale, devotes only 46 percent of its square footage to usable space. Table 1 illustrates the differences among the presidential libraries in amount of usable space in relation to gross square footage. The table further notes how much of the gross square footage is devoted to each of the major library functions.

The committee report recommends that the archivist promulgate agency regulations to provide for the maximum amount of usable space, subject to environmental and security requirements. The archivist noted that the National Archives and Records Service has already developed guidelines for the planning and design of presidential libraries. These guidelines do not have the force of agency regulations, but they are persuasive and have already been employed in planning the Carter Library, which, in Warner's words, has "resulted in a building that will be compact and efficient."[9] The guidelines describe comprehensively the types of space required by the library, the relationships of different spaces, and the size of spaces. Further, they record the kind of activities performed in the various departments and work areas, the number and categories of visitors, the volume of traffic expected, and the traffic patterns. They also stress the need for environmental control and security provisions. Judith A. Koucky, an archivist in the Office of Presidential Libraries, notes that: "The 'guidelines' discussed in the preceding paragraph and alluded to by individuals taking part in the hearings on H.R. 3138 are in a document written by the Office of Presidential Libraries and entitled *General Requirements for a Presidential Library Building.*"

"Whenever a new Presidential Library is being developed, the Office of Presidential Libraries draws up requirements that meet the particular needs of that Library. These specifications are then appended to the *General Requirements* document and are given to the architect."[10]

The statement developed in the *General Requirements* document "is intended to provide architectural planners with the basic information on the nature of the structure needed to serve the functions of a Presidential Library. It is intended primarily as an outline of general considerations to be kept in mind by architects, rather than as a detailed statement of requirements."[11] With the help of these guidelines, an architect should be able to plan a library that will be functional, economical to operate, and attractive and will meet the needs of the clientele for whom it is intended.

ENDOWMENTS AND OTHER GIFTS

The general services administrator is authorized by the Presidential Libraries Act to accept private bequests and donations for the operation of a library.[12] Private citizens have generously responded to the opportunity of lending their support and formed nonprofit support organizations in conjunction with each of the presidential libraries.[13] In 1982, these organizations spent over $1 million to advance the work of the libraries.

In order to reduce the cost of maintaining the libraries, a number of legislators have favored making endowments mandatory rather than leaving it completely to the private groups' discretion whether to collect funds, when to collect them, and how to use them. The archivist has observed that there are limitations as to the areas for which endowments can be required. He stresses that the Presidential Records Act stipulates that the government receive and retain complete ownership, possession, and control of presidential records starting with those created during the term of office beginning January 20, 1981.

The Presidential Records Act requires that the archivist deposit the records in a presidential library or another archival facility. To meet this obligation, the archivist must perform a number of core functions, and the U.S. government must provide the means to enable the archivist to fulfill this responsibility. Beyond the core functions are ancillary functions that are not indispensable for the operation of the library and therefore need not be performed by the government. Some functions lie in a grey area and may be assumed by the government or by a private group.

To clarify the characteristics of these three categories, some typical functions for each may be listed:

> Core functions: Maintenance and operation of building; provision of security and proper environmental conditions; acquisition, arrangement and description of materials; museum exhibits; staff training.
>
> Functions performed by supporting groups: Obtaining funds for library building.
>
> Functions that may be performed by either government or supporting groups: Oral history projects; museum projects, in particular ambitious projects; other functions generally not considered essential.

The administrator has the authority to require the establishment of an endowment as a precondition for forwarding a presidential library proposal to Congress, which must approve library proposals. Several endowment options have been suggested:

1. The endowment may cover all or a specified cost of operating a library.
2. An endowment of a predetermined size may be established.
3. The endowment may cover the cost of operating and maintaining that part of a building exceeding a predetermined size.
4. The endowment may fund programs and activities not included among specified core functions of the library.

The "Endowments for Presidential Libraries" report finds that the negative aspects of options 1–3 are so significant that they should not be pursued; the report favors option 4. Use of option 4 would allow the archivist to state clearly those activities that should be performed by private groups, by the former president, or by his supporters.[14]

In accordance with this view, the archivist did not favor the endowment provisions of House bill 1349 of the ninety-ninth Congress, accompanied by House report 99–125.[15]

PRESIDENTIAL LIBRARIES ACT OF 1986

In spite of the reservations stated in House report 99–125, House bill 1349 was passed. It was approved by the president on May 28, 1986, and became public law 99–323, the Presidential Libraries Act of 1986. It is designed to reduce the cost of operating presidential libraries.

According to this law, the archivist may, when he considers it in the public interest, accept for and in the name of the United States land, a facility, and equipment. He may also enter into agreement with a university, other institution of higher learning, institute, or foundation to use as an archival depository, land, a facility, and equipment, accept for and in the name of the United States gifts to be used for making any physical and material change in a presidential archival depository.

Prior to accepting land, facility, or equipment or prior to entering into agreement with a university or other institutions, the archivist must describe in a detailed report to Congress the items intended to be donated or made available for use, the scope of the anticipated collection, and the anticipated annual cost. Similar scrutiny applies to gifts for making any physical and material change. The plans must meet the standards developed by the archivist.

The archivist may also solicit gifts for the purpose of maintaining, operating, protecting, and improving a presidential archival depository. Probably the most important provision of the law concerns endowments. The law stipulates that the archivist shall not accept land, facility, or equipment or enter into an agreement to use land, facility, or equipment for the purpose of creating a presidential archival facility unless there is provided an amount for the purpose of maintaining such facility equal to:

(A) the product of—
(i) the total cost of acquiring or constructing such facility and of acquiring and installing such equipment, multiplied by
(ii) 20 percent; plus
(B) (i) if title to the land is to be vested in the United States, the product of—
(I) the total cost of acquiring the land upon which such facility is located, or such other measure of the value of such land as is mutually agreed upon by the Archivist and the donor, multiplied by
(II) 20 percent; or

(ii) if title to the land is not to be vested in the United States, the product of—

(I) the total cost to the donor of any improvements to the land upon which such facility is located (other than such facility and equipment), multiplied by

(II) 20 percent; plus

(C) if the Presidential archival depository will exceed 70,000 square feet in area, an amount equal to the product of—

(i) the sum of—

(I) the total cost described in clause (i) of subparagraph (A); plus

(II) the total cost described in subclause (I) or (II) of subparagraph (B)(i), as the case may be, multiplied by "(ii) the percentage obtained by dividing the number of square feet by which such depository will exceed 70,000 square feet by 70,000.[16]

A similar 20 percent endowment provision applies if a proposed physical or material change would result in an increase in the cost of the operation of the facility.

It is evident that the framers of the law wish to keep the size of the new archival depositories below 70,000 square feet by imposing higher endowment requirements for the square footage exceeding 70,000 square feet.

The law is applicable only to Presidential archival depositories created for presidents who take office for the first time on or after January 29, 1985. In other words, the law does not apply to former President Richard Nixon, for whom a library has not yet been established, or to Ronald Reagan.

Public law 99–323 further charges the archivist to undertake— in consultation with the secretary of the Smithsonian Institution and the National Capitol Planning Commission—a study to explore the demand for a museum of the presidents and to investigate costs and space and program requirements for such a museum. The study should examine the feasibility of establishing the museum exclusively with nonfederal funds.

NOTES

1. U.S. Congress, House, Committee on Government Operations, *To Provide for the Acceptance of Presidential Libraries and for Other Purposes: Hearing on H.J. Res. 330, H.J. Res. 331 and H.J. Res. 332*, 84th Cong., 1st sess., 1955, pp. 29–30.

2. U.S. Congress, House, Committee on Government Operations, *Presidential Libraries Funding: Hearing on H.R. 3138 and Related Bills*, 98th Cong., 2d sess., 1984, p. 75.

3. Judith A. Koucky, archivist, Office of Presidential Libraries, Letter to author, June 6, 1986.

4. For instance: *Presidential Libraries Funding*; U.S. Congress, Senate, Commmittee on Governmental Affairs, *Former Presidents Facilities and Services Reform Act of 1983: Report, together with Minority Views to Accompany S.563*, 98th Cong., 2d sess., 1984, S.Rept. 98–637; U.S. Congress, House, *Reduction of Costs of Presidential Libraries: Report to Accompany H.R. 1349*, 99th Cong., 1st sess., 1985, H.Rept. 99–125.

5. *To Provide for the Acceptance*, pp. 10–12, 29–31.

6. *Presidential Libraries Funding*, pp. 103–16, 146–48, and 68–72.

7. Ibid., pp. 108–9.

8. The following information is based largely on U.S. Congress, House, Committee on Government Operations, *Reduction of Costs of Presidential Libraries: Report to Accompany H.R. 1349*, 99th Cong., 1st sess., 1985, H.Rept. 99–125, esp. pp. 6–9.

9. *Presidential Libraries Funding*, p. 53.

10. Judith A. Koucky, archivist, Office of Presidential Libraries, Letter to author, February 14, 1986.

11. U.S. National Archives, Office of Presidential Libraries, *General Requirements for a Presidential Library Building* (n.d.), p. 1.

12. The information in this section is based largely on the "Endowments for Presidential Libraries" report in *Presidential Libraries Funding*, pp. 159–73.

13. These organizations are described in chapter 4 and appendix 3.

14. Ibid., pp. 167–70.

15. This bill and the accompanying report are practically identical with H.R. 5584, 98th Cong., accompanied by H.Rept., 98–856. H.R. 1349 had to be introduced since H.R. 5584 was permitted to die in the preceding Congress.

16. U.S. Code Title 4, sec. 2112g (3)(A) to (C) as amended by public law 99–323.

3

Archival Depository and Other Topics

WHAT CONSTITUTES AN ARCHIVAL DEPOSITORY?

The general services administrator has been given considerable leeway in determining what constitutes an archival depository. That he has interpreted his authority in a flexible fashion can be illustrated by arrangements among the General Services Administration, presidential libraries, and the National Park Service. In the case of the Roosevelt Library, the library, the home, and the gravesite are in Hyde Park, New York, on the same estate. The Roosevelt Library and Museum is operated and maintained by the National Archives; the home and gravesite are maintained by the Park Service. The Hoover Library in West Branch, Iowa, is operated by the National Archives. The Hoover home and the other buildings are operated by the Park Service. A different pattern has been chosen for the Eisenhower Library located in Abilene, Kansas. This library is on the same grounds as the Eisenhower home, museum, visitors center, and place of meditation—all operated and maintained by the National Archives. The Ford Library and the Ford Museum are not only in different buildings but also in different cities—the library in Ann Arbor, Michigan, the museum in Grand Rapids, Michigan. Both facilities are operated by the National Archives.[1]

NATURE OF PRESIDENTIAL PAPERS

The question of the nature of the presidential papers has been clearly answered by two White House officials in charge of the White House Files Unit for many years, William J. Hopkins and William F. Matthews.[2] Also helpful in finding an answer to the question is the National Study Commission Report, which devoted a section to the nature of presidential papers.[3] The following discussion relies largely on these sources.

A firm classification system for the presidential papers was developed during the first administration of Franklin D. Roosevelt. Frank Matthews established a scheme consisting of sixty-one subject categories, broken down into chronological and numerical divisions. During the Kennedy administration, he wrote the Central Files Manual.

The main file unit is the White House Central Files, which receives and classifies files, maintains them, and retrieves upon request the documents generated and received by the White House.

Material in Central Files consists of incoming correspondence processed by the White House mailrooms and copies of outgoing correspondence, reports, memoranda, and similar material generated or received by the Office of the President and the various White House Staff offices. Many of the incoming correspondence consists of letters to the president from private citizens, but it also includes letters from state and federal officials, including memers of Congress; letters from officials of foreign countries; and letters addressed to officials of the White House other than the president. Drafts of memoranda, speeches, correspondence, and so on prepared by officials other than the president are generally filed with Central Files. Drafts of such documents that are handwritten by the president generally are not retained in Central Files.

Correspondence and records of the Domestic Council and the Council on International Economic Policy are filed in the Central Files.[4]

The National Security Council, an agency within the Executive Office of the President, maintains two categories of files: institutional files and noninstitutional, or presidential acquisition files.

Institutional files contain such material as National Security Council study and decision memoranda, reports, and recommendations prepared for the council. These materials are retained by the council and remain with the council from administration to administration, since they are considered federal records.

Noninstitutional, or presidential acquisitions, files consist of briefing materials for the president, correspondence with foreign heads of state or governments, and correspondence with directives to agencies within the executive branch dealing with foreign affairs. These files, though maintained by the National Security Council staff, are not treated as federal records and can be removed by the president at the conclusion of his term of office.

Most other bodies within the Executive Office of the President maintain their own filing systems. With regard to them, the White House Central Files receive only their correspondence and transmissions into the president's office and copies of the transmissions from the president's office to these bodies.

In general, records of agencies that are mainly advisory are treated as presidential records. The treatment of agencies and their records has not been uniform and consistent through the years, and the line of demarcation between advisory and administrative has not been rigid.[5]

Several recent presidents have maintained special files, which usually contain highly sensitive materials. Truman's private secretary included in a special file communications between Truman and foreign heads of state, papers regarding the seizure of the steel industry, and civil rights. During the Nixon administration, the White House staff secretary's office kept a special file that contained investigative reports, documents concerning personal affairs of individuals, and material that might be prejudicial to the national interest.

In Ford's administration, the special files unit was abolished, but Ford's secretary kept a file consisting of important materials, including a special section with sensitive materials.

The presidents following Franklin D. Roosevelt considered the papers created by members of their staff as presidential papers; however, the presidents could not always exercise adequate control, and they did not always succeed in their efforts to have the assistants turn over the materials to them.

Files of White House ancillary offices contain the papers accumulated by such offices as the White House Social Office, the White House Telephone Office, and the White House Reporter.

The White House Central Files Unit maintains the permanent file. It consists of materials of a precedential nature—therefore also called Precedential File—and useful to subsequent administrations when dealing with certain internal White House situations. An example is the procedure followed in designing a flag when new states are admitted to the Union.

LIAISON BETWEEN WHITE HOUSE AND NATIONAL ARCHIVES

While still in office, a number of presidents welcomed assistance from the National Archives in preparing papers and other matérials for their pojected presidential library. President Truman requested general services administrator Jeff Larson to provide two archivists to assist him with work on his papers. This request was granted. It was understood that the papers would be turned over to the government later.[6]

During the Johnson administration, a member of the White House staff was placed on the National Archives payroll and began preparing materials for the Johnson Library. For instance, she transferred Johnson's congressional papers from the files of the House and Senate to the National Archives, she compiled information about memorabilia, and she kept a diary of daily visitors. Nixon followed Johnson's example and asked that an office similar to that established for Johnson be continued.

In the Nixon presidency, the office developed a daily diary of the president's meetings, telephone conversations, and movements, and it identified major and minor figures in photographs taken by White House photographers. By 1972, the office, called the Office of Presidential Papers and Archives, had grown to twelve members. It remained at this strength until 1974 when President Nixon resigned.

The services of such a liaison office were subsequently offered to Presidents Ford and Carter. Ford declined; Carter accepted. The staff provided for Carter assembled a book collection and a clipping file on the Carter presidency, helped pack and store White House gifts, conducted exit interviews and oral history interviews with members of Carter's family, and in general worked with the White House in achieving a good record-keeping practice.[7]

At present there is no official liaison staff between the White House and the National Archives. The Office of Presidential Libraries maintains, however, close contact with White House officials responsible for managing current presidential records and receiving presidential gifts.[8]

Liaison activities between the National Archives and the White House have been fruitful. The Liaison Office, consisting of several members, can offer extensive, systematic help; informal arrangements can also be productive. The goal of formal and informal procedures is assistance in managing current records and in preparing and organizing materials for their eventual transfer to a projected presidential library. The materials will thus become more speedily available for use once the library is in operation.

INTERPRETING DATA

Larry S. Berman gives some practical advice about interpreting data held by presidential libraries.[9] He deplores their unevenness and the problem of verification. He emphasizes that special care must be taken in assessing the value of oral history interviews since the interviewer may present data in a slant favorable to himself or to his friends. As Berman further notes, written memoranda too must be evaluated as to their significance and trustworthiness. Do they give a correct picture of the influence of an adviser? For instance, adviser A may not be able or may not wish to see the president. He therefore addresses numerous memos to the president. Adviser B, on the other hand, has the ear of the president and easy access to his office. He can convey his views orally, in person. To use Berman's illustration, as against twenty memos of adviser A, the files show only one memo from adviser B. Berman therefore suggests always to triangulate the data, checking source against source, comparing official documentation with personal interviews, memoirs, texts, and other types of material.

Besides the many memoirs that reveal or verify significant historical records, some materials may seem slight and perhaps even embarrassing to the president. An archivist would not withhold them from an interested user of presidential materials unless there were an acknowledged reason for restricting access. Berman, who has closely examined the materials in the Johnson Library, found among them a number of stories that, though "less than analytically useful," are highly quotable and helpful in revealing aspects of Johnson's personality.

One of the stories concerns budget director Kermit Gordon. President Johnson is said to have tried to reach him on the telephone. Gordon could not be found, so the story goes, because he had gone to a concert. The next morning Johnson is said to have called Gordon and asked "Well, playboy, did you have a good time last night?" Regarding this matter Gordon wrote to Bill Moyers:

If you are keeping score on the press stories portraying the President as a man who constantly abuses his staff, you might want to have [this memo] for the record. . . . The incident never occurred. Moreover, in all the time I worked for President Johnson, I suffered but a single mild rebuke—much milder than the circumstances would have justified.[10]

Another story refers to an "important" memo:

Mr. Bryant came by to say that he is sending Yuki [the dog] out to Walter Reed to be dipped and treated for fleas he got in Texas. Mr. Bryant has tried everything he has, and Yuki is still scratching. He will stay at Walter Reed's until 1:30 P.M. Friday.[11]

WEEDING

Archivists recognize that the rejection of some papers offered as gifts and the disposal of some papers already part of a collection is necessary to keep a collection focused on its objectives and to keep it within manageable bounds.[12] The presidential libraries have not been exempt from this need to prevent unchecked growth by eliminating materials of no archival value. One category of materials—the exchange of correspondence between the president and the citizenry—has been subject to continuing appraisal because of its steady growth. David J. Reed, a former assistant archivist for presidential libraries, speaks to this subject.[13]

According to Reed, President Roosevelt received an average of 140,000 letters per year. During the Kennedy administration, the number increased to 300,000 and under President Johnson to more than 800,000. In 1977 Carter received over 3 million letters, and it was expected that he would receive between 1 1/2 and 2 million in 1978. According to Clarence E. Henley, President Reagan receives about 65,000 letters a week, which would yield over 3 million items a year.[14]

Reed observes that disposal of relatively large amounts of such material occurs as a matter of routine. For instance, the Carter White House disposed of bulk mail consisting of letters answered by form replies, unacknowledged letters, and other letters that did not warrant a reply. Such materials had been accumulating at the rate of approximately 1,000 cubic feet every six months.[15]

The Reagan White House, which receives about 65,000 letters a week, follows a disposal schedule after action has been completed in accordance with the Presidential Records Act. Clarence E. Henley reports that the archivist of the United States has so far authorized the destruction of some 10,000 cubic feet of this material, although a sample has been retained for researchers.[16]

Disposal of presidential materials began with earlier administrations. For instance, in 1952, unacknowledged public opinion mail to President Truman was sampled by the National Arhives staff, and about 200 square feet were destroyed. In 1976, upon approval by the Office of Presidential Libraries, the Roosevelt Library carried out a plan to dispose of the alphabetical file of public correspondence to the White House during Roosevelt's term of office; only a systematic random sample of this file has been retained. The files that were removed occupied about 25 percent of the Roosevelt Library and offered practically no research information.[17]

COMPUTER USE

The presidential libraries system intends to keep pace with advances in the communications technology. This is evident from plans disclosed by James E. O'Neill, assistant archivist for presidential libraries. He stated in an interview that the projected Carter presidential library will include a significant quantity of machine-readable documents that will necessitate use of computers by the researchers. Beyond this, there is a plan to use computers in presidential libraries for housekeeping jobs and, in particular, for the preparation of finding aids.[18]

As to the current status of computerization in presidential libraries, the author received this information, which he reproduces with some slight changes.

The Office of Presidential Libraries has completed a feasibility study and the preliminary design of a manuscript processing and reference system. The prototype of the system is being built on a Prime Model 2250, a 32-bit minicomputer for distributed processing application. The prototype model was tested at the Ford Library during April and May 1986. After completion of the task, the Office of Presidential Libraries will decide how the system is to be implemented in all presidential libraries.

The system is designed to provide automated assistance throughout the archival cycle—from solicitation through use of the acquired materials. Information noted during the solicitation and acquisitions phase will be utilized in the more detailed descriptions of the description and arrangement phases. Uniform subject descriptors will be used for the identification of each series and file folder to allow automated searching of the data base.

After the system has been installed in each library, all libraries will be linked through a central data base containing the finding aids of all libraries. Each of the libraries thus can undertake searches of the holdings of all libraries in the system.[19] Use can be extended by making the data base available to archives and libraries not part of the presidential libraries—for instance, university libraries. A user could then consult finding aids in his or her home town to help determine whether a trip to a library might prove fruitful.[20]

NOTES

1. U.S. Congress, House, Committee on Government Operations, *Presidential Libraries: Unexplored Funding Alternatives*, Thirtieth Report of the Committee, 97th Cong., 2d sess., 1982, H. Rept. 97–732, pp. 7–8.

2. William J. Hopkins, executive assistant to the president, affidavit deposed in the U.S. District Court for the District of Columbia. Richard Nixon, plaintiff, v. Administrator of General Services . . . , Defendants, June 30, 1975, civil action no. 74–1852; William F. Matthews, chief of White House Central Files Unit, affidavit deposed in the U.S. District Court for the District Court for the District of Columbia, Richard Nixon, plaintiff, v. Administrator of General Services . . . , Defendants, July 7, 1975, civil action no. 74–1852.

3. "Final Report of the National Study Commission on Records and Documents of Federal Officials, March 31, 1977, *in* U.S. Congress, House, Committee on Government Operations, *Presidential Records Act of 1978: Hearings on H.R. 10998 and Related Bills*, 95th Cong., 2d sess., 1978, pp. 440–41.

4. Matthews, affidavit, Mimeographed copy, pp. 1–2.

5. *Presidential Records Act of 1978*, p. 440.

6. U.S. Congress, Senate, Committee on Government Operations, *GSA Regulations Implementing Presidential Recordings and Materials Preservation Act: Hearing*, 94th Cong., 1st sess., 1975, p. 252.

7. Raymond H. Geselbrecht and Daniel J. Reed, "The Presidential Library and the White House Liaison Office," *American Archivist* 46, no. 1 (Winter 1983): 69–72. See also Robert M. Warner, testimony in U.S. Congress, House, Committee on Government Operations, *Presidential Libraries Funding: Hearing on H.R. 3138 and Related Bills*, 98th Cong., 2d sess., 1984, pp. 59–60; and James E. O'Neill, "Will Success Spoil the Presidential Libraries," *American Archivist* 36, no. 3 (July 1973): 343–44.

8. Judith A. Koucky, archivist, Office of Presidential Libraries, Letter to author, February 14, 1986.

9. Larry Berman, "The Evolution and Value of Presidential Libraries," in Harold C. Relyea et al., *The Presidency and Information Policy* (New York: Center for the Study of the Presidency, 1981), Proceedings v.iv, no. 1, 1981), pp. 88–90.

10. Kermit Gordon Letter to Bill Moyers, July 28, 1965, executive/FS 11–1, Container 11, folder June 13, 1965-August 19, 1965, quoted in ibid., pp. 88–89, 160.

11. Mary R., memorandum to the president, June 5, 1968, diary backup, June 5, 1968, quoted in ibid., pp. 89, 160.

12. For a wide-ranging discussion of records disposition, including appraisal, deaccessioning, and destruction, see Nancy E. Peace, ed., *Archival Choices: The Historical Record in an Age of Abundance* (Lexington, Mass.: Lexington Books, 1984). See especially the chapters by Nancy E. Ham, John Dejka and Sheila Conner, Patricia Aronson, Lawrence Dowler, and F. Gerald Ham.

13. D. J. Reed, "A Matter of Size: The Paper Problem in Two Branches of Government," *in Presidential Records Act of 1978*, pp. 749–55.

14. Clarence E. Henley, director, Office of Records Management, Letter to author, July 2, 1985.

15. Reed, "Matter of Size," p. 750.

16. Henley, Letter to author.

17. Reed, "Matter of Size," p. 750.

18. Joseph Deitch, "Portrait: James O'Neill," *Wilson Library Bulletin* 59, no. 7 (March 1985): 479–81.

19. Judith A. Koucky, archivist, Office of Presidential Libraries, Letters to author, February 20, June 3, 1986.

20. Deitch, "Portrait," pp. 480–81.

4

The Presidential Libraries
Viewed as a Group

HOLDINGS

There has been a steady increase in the creation of presidential papers from presidency to presidency. Table 2 reveals that with the exception of the Carter materials project, all institutions hold federal records, with Johnson's leading the group. In addition to federal records in their original form, Johnson has large quantities of federal records on microfilm.

All libraries have audiovisual materials. The Carter still picture collection is by far the largest. The film collections vary greatly, Kennedy outdistancing all others, followed in descending order by these libraries and projects: Nixon, Carter, Johnson, Eisenhower, Truman, Roosevelt, and Hoover.

The book holdings vary greatly. Books are not the chief component in presidential library materials that they are in traditional libraries. As compared to their holdings of papers, book collections of

Table 2
Accessions and Holdings

	HOOVER	ROOSEVELT	TRUMAN	EISENHOWER
I. ACCESSIONS & HOLDINGS				
PAPERS (Pages)				
Personal Papers	6,470,789	15,940,901	13,200,824	18,970,440
Federal Records	108,130	716,000	675,600	631,700
Presidential Records	0	0	0	0
MICROFORMS (Rolls/Cards)				
Personal Papers	701	657	3,221	935
Federal Records	663	13	32	0
Presidential Records	0	0	1	0
AUDIOVISUAL				
Still Pictures (Images)	32,280	130,212	81,901	188,284
Film (Feet)	151,591	309,476	323,624	601,145
Video Tape (Hours)	14	28	56	19
Audio Tape (Hours)	238	1,024	255	876
Audio Discs (Hours)	71	1,107	239	232
ORAL HISTORY				
Pages	11,017	3,120	44,350	29,987
Hours	0	84	1,301	750
MUSEUM OBJECTS	4,420	23,159	21,047	28,022
PRINTED MATERIALS				
Books (Volumes)	24,279	44,538	44,800	21,728
Serials	26,991	32,733	74,856	34,082
Microform	1,401	2,239	3,681	5,126
Other	1,307	85,828	89,565	23,674

Source: Office of Presidential Libraries.

presidential libraries are small. The Kennedy Library has the largest collection, followed in descending order by the Truman, Roosevelt, and Hoover libraries. The collections of these three libraries are of approximately the same size; they are followed by the Eisenhower, Johnson, Nixon, Ford, and Carter libraries.

Oral history has been a favored device for reinforcing or weakening, as the case may be, objective historical data. So far, oral history projects have been carried out more widely by the older presidential libraries. Only a few oral history interviews have been administered by the Ford and Carter libraries; the Johnson, Truman, Kennedy, and Eisenhower libraries have administered a larger number.

RESEARCHER VISITS AND MUSEUM VISITORS

The use made of the presidential libraries is one of the most important indicators of the value of the libraries to society. The presidential libraries attract people for various reasons. Researchers investigate historically significant documents. Museum visitors

Table 2
Continued

KENNEDY	JOHNSON	NIXON	FORD	CARTER	TOTAL HOLDINGS TO DATE
25,396,832	24,955,582	784,000	16,345,517	26,000,880	148,065,765
629,800	2,836,320	912,000	242,000	0	6,751,550
4,000	0	44,414,000	0	131,000	44,549,000
447	572,729	0	23	0	578,713
1,972	5,962,000	0	0	0	5,964,680
0	0	5,312	0	0	5,313
125,855	599,530	435,000	308,059	1,500,000	3,401,121
6,977,872	824,743	2,200,000	65,200	1,120,080	12,573,731
975	5,996	3,900	1,013	1,434	13,435
6,810	11,645	1,490	961	2,000	25,299
704	782	0	1	0	3,136
35,711	47,921	2,200	173	606	175,085
1,618	2,119	228	0	148	6,248
14,630	37,421	21,750	3,120	40,000	193,569
70,310	14,896	9,000	8,576	1,021	239,148
11,685	3,727	0	39	2,152	186,265
3,873	3,248	0	0	5,969	25,537
9,941	10,015	0	1,437	5,756	227,523

come primarily to view the museum objects and the building. They usually spend one day or part of one day on the premises and its surroundings; researchers often stay several days or even weeks and make repeated visits.

Visits by researchers and visits by museum visitors are recorded in different ways. Each visit by a museum visitor is credited to a separate individual. In the case of researchers, visits as such are counted without establishing whether they represent multiple visits by the same person.

There are considerable differences among the libraries in use by researchers and by museum visitors (tables 3 and 4). In 1985 the Johnson Library had the largest number of research visits, followed rather closely by the Kennedy Library. In descending order, these libraries follow: Truman, Roosevelt, Ford, Eisenhower, and Hoover. The picture is similar for the number of museum visitors. Again, the list is topped by the Johnson Library, in descending order joined by the Kennedy, Roosevelt, Truman, Eisenhower, Ford, and Hoover libraries.

The differences among the libraries as to the number of visits

Table 3
Presidential Libraries Museum Visitors, 1947–1985

Fiscal Year	Hoover	Roosevelt	Truman	Eisenhower	Kennedy	Johnson	Ford	Total
1947-1961		3,005,289						3,005,289
1958-1961			474,555					474,555
1962		138,802	150,161	131,000				419,963
1963		161,190	140,538	106,792				408,520
1964	39,362	161,469	155,053	101,988				457,872
1965	78,857	177,537	179,890	91,891				528,175
1966	95,713	180,915	193,045	93,496				563,169
1967	73,577	159,363	180,824	139,427				553,191
1968	81,056	157,116	170,671	148,179				557,022
1969	80,751	164,298	165,384	364,750				775,183
1970	91,083	162,423	182,823	449,631				885,960
1971	70,648	160,295	186,174	263,234		85,240		765,591
1972	81,989	181,520	186,866	318,684		676,116		1,445,175
1973	82,822	191,194	340,818	299,741		704,190		1,618,765
1974	84,002	194,314	264,230	215,586		542,717		1,300,849
1975	106,109	188,106	291,180	197,727		520,985		1,304,107
1976 & TQ	148,099	223,673	510,584	295,532		905,244		2,083,132
1977	91,324	371,514	321,136	177,332		657,907		1,619,213
1978	95,418	276,865	264,714	170,172		502,115		1,309,284
1979	69,775	215,582	219,067	127,026		480,521		1,111,971
1980	64,088	241,459	201,642	143,910	563,470	446,062		1,660,631
1981	70,337	226,238	211,864	125,458	358,554	384,884	22,476	1,399,811
1982	61,227	202,048	197,477	131,961	318,845	368,289	423,886	1,703,733
1983	59,637	206,147	200,913	117,420	255,474	409,304	83,071	1,331,966
1984	58,487	186,833	210,149	109,720	283,568	357,390	139,529	1,345,676
1985	50,310	194,578	188,552	115,103	252,617	402,768	114,214	1,318,142
TOTAL	1,734,671	7,728,768	5,788,310	4,435,760	2,032,528	7,443,732	783,176	29,946,945

Note: In fiscal year 1976 there was an extra transition quarter, which changed the beginning of the fiscal years thereafter from July 1 to October 1.
Source: Office of Presidential Libraries.

44

Table 4
Presidential Libraries Researcher Visits, 1946–1985[1]

Fiscal Year	Hoover	Roosevelt	Truman	Eisenhower	Kennedy	Johnson	Nixon	Ford	Carter	Total
1946–1964		9,341								9,341
1958–1964			2,217							2,217
1965		669	794							1,463
1966	41	862	514	12						1,429
1967	225	1,089	603	97						2,014
1968	327	1,094	921	35						2,377
1969	452	1,066	826	99						2,443
1970	598	1,112	996	144	36					2,886
1971	509	1,192	808	209	316					3,034
1972	563	1,604	283	173	389	185				3,197
1973	609	1,345	767	342	461	484				4,008
1974	616	1,278	1,051	336	868	1,116				5,265
1975	498	1,361	880	390	682	1,243				5,054
1976 & TQ	949	2,274	1,663	756	957	1,564				8,163
1977	427	1,303	886	484	1,123	1,297				5,520
1978	528	1,535	985	496	878	1,797				6,219
1979	958	1,097	785	527	785	1,533		122		5,807
1980	614	1,603	973	625	1,419	1,618	84	119		7,055
1981	672	1,243	1,306	676	2,975	1,687	121	74		8,754
1982	686	1,439	918	648	2,196	2,257	124	234		8,502
1983	656	1,283	1,378	802	2,251	1,848	87	496		8,801
1984	582	1,415	1,361	718	2,251	1,804	259	863		9,253
1985	604	1,016	1,211	748	2,110	2,301	852	977		9,819
TOTAL	11,114	36,221	22,126	8,317	19,697	20,734	1,527	2,885		122,621

[1]Total number of days all researchers visited research rooms.
Note: In 1976 there was an extra transition quarter, which changed the beginning of the fiscal years thereafter from July 1 to October 1.
Source: Office of Presidential Libraries.

(researcher visits and museum visitors) are significantly reduced if such visits are spread over a five-year span (figures 3 and 4).

An examination of tables 3 and 4 shows that the rank order among the libraries as to the number of visitors has been changing over the years. An attempt to establish the reasons for these changes would go beyond the scope of our study. It would, however, be interesting to isolate the factors that contribute to the popularity of a library. Factors that should play an important role, among others, are size of collection, research potential, general research interest in a president, date of establishment, kind of collection, size of collection, location, finding aids, and staff assistance.

ACQUISITION OF MATERIALS

Materials are acquired on the basis of an acquisition program developed within the framework of guidelines applicable to all presidential libraries.[1] In shaping the program, the director of the library works in cooperation with the assistant archivist for presidential libraries, whose approval of the program is required.

Items are acquired with the intention that they become a permanent part of the collection. The acquisition of materials is based on a sequence determined by priorities appropriate to a particular library.

The materials sought may be in many forms: textual, audiovisual, three-dimensional, and machine-readable. The decisive factor is the content, not the form. The materials must have some subject matter or physical relationship to the former president. It is important to note again that the materials are not limited to those produced or received during the former president's tenure as president.

The core holdings consist of the historical materials donated by the president and materials received under the provisions of the Presidential Records Act of 1978 or other laws. Beyond the core holdings, the library seeks collateral historical materials from family, close friends, political, governmental, and social associates, and political opponents.

Library staff members are cautioned not to offend prospective donors. Although only historically significant materials having a bearing on the former president's life and career are wanted, it is sometimes advisable for the library to accept unsolicited materials even if they are of marginal value or even unsuitable for the collection. The library might accept such items if the refusal might offend the would-be donor or damage the library's public relations.

All transfers of materials to a presidential library must be supported by deeds of gift or other appropriate legal documentation.

Figure 3
Presidential Libraries Museum Visitors, 1981–1985

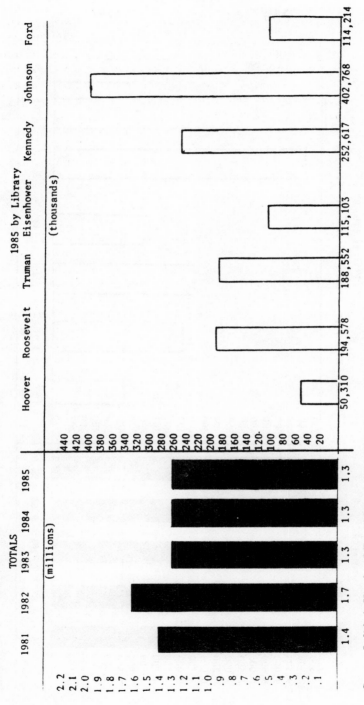

Source: Judith A. Koucky, Office of Presidential Libraries.

Figure 4
Presidential Libraries Researcher Visits, 1981–1985

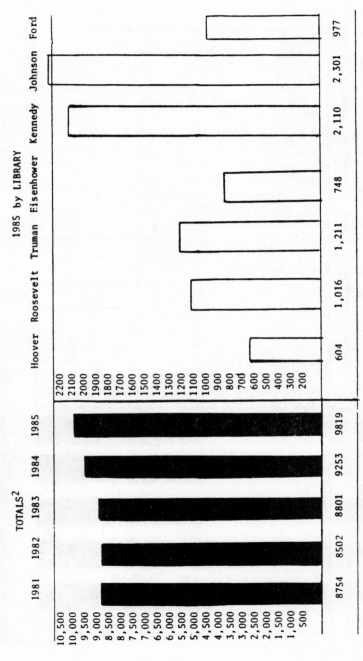

[1]Totals include special access researchers in Nixon materials.
Note: Total number of days all researchers visited research rooms.
Source: Judith A. Koucky, Office of Presidential Libraries.

Since there are differences in the formulation and execution of the programs, several programs are discussed in the descriptions of individual libraries. See especially the descriptions in the next chapter of the Roosevelt Library, the Kennedy Library, and the Carter Materials Project.

STAFFS OF PRESIDENTIAL LIBRARIES

The Office of Personnel Management (OPM), in cooperation with the National Archives and Records Service, establishes the staff categories for the National Archives as it does for all other branches of the federal civil service. In consultation with the Archives, the OPM works out the qualifications for the various job categories and grade levels. As in the entire National Archives and Records Service, archivist and archives technician are the two kinds of positions most prevalent in the presidential libraries.[2]

The flexible requirements for becoming an archivist stress an academic background and professional experience, which in combination provide the knowledge for the solution of professional archival problems. Emphasized are courses in U.S. history, political science, U.S. government, U.S. civilization, economics, and public administration.

For technician positions, the applicant must possess experience of a clerical, supervisory, or administrative nature gained in archival or related work, such as experience as a library technical assistant. A specified amount and kind of study beyond high school may be substituted for experience.

New appointments in the professional category of archivist occur at the GS–7 and GS–9 levels. Archivists with extensive experience, advanced academic background, and commensurate professional responsibilities can reach levels extending to GS–14, and in rare instances beyond.

Most paraprofessional staff members enter at the GS–4 and GS–5 levels, depending on experience or extent of study beyond high school. The full performance level is GS–6. There are only limited opportunities for technicians to move beyond this level.

The directors of the presidential libraries select the individuals on their staff. Directors follow a staffing pattern that has been approved by the Office of Presidential libraries. This pattern takes into account the size and activities of a library at its particular stage of development. There are typical patterns. For instance, the Eisenhower Library staff pattern is that of a typical mature library. The approval of a library's staffing pattern by the Office of Presidential Libraries is a very important prerogative of this office. Approval of the staff pattern means that the Office of Presidential Libraries determines number and type of staff members for each presidential library.

An examination of the questionnaire returns reveals that the various libraries have been given considerable leeway in selecting the kind of staff they find useful for their particular operations. While most members of the professional staff are archivists, each Library also has specialists who can deal with a library's particular concerns and interests, such as exhibits and other museum activities.

SUPPORTING ORGANIZATIONS

All presidential library buildings have been erected with private resources. Once established, the libraries usually continue to benefit from private organizations formed to support the libraries' programs. As stated by the Office of Presidential Libraries, in several instances, the organizations "evolved from bodies chartered to raise money and construct the original library structure or an addition to it. In other cases, these organizations were established by friends of the president or his family or by interested members of the community in which the library is located."[3]

The organization and operation of these supporting organizations may take various forms:

> Some of the organizations encourage contributing public membership through payment of membership fees. Others are non-membership charitable foundations or corporations. Some seek grants from foundations or Government bodies to carry on their work. Others seek to support their activities solely through private contributions. Several of the organizations are run by paid staff members. Others are totally voluntary. Boards of directors of the organizations may include interested members of the community, family and friends of the President, his political or public associates, or representatives of the scholarly or academic community. In some cases, the library directors hold official or ex-officio positions on the organizations' boards of directors.[4]

These organizations support a host of programs, mainly activities for which public funds may not be obtainable:

> Programs of Presidential libraries' supporting organizations include providing grants-in-aid to scholars performing research work in the libraries, sponsoring scholarly conferences concerning the Presidents and their eras, underwriting costs of new or traveling exhibits in the libraries' museums, publishing scholarly and popular works concern-

ing the Presidents and their administrations, assisting the libraries to acquire historical materials, sponsoring social events to generate support for the libraries, and supporting any programs of the libraries for which Federal funds may not be available, including oral history projects. Charters of several of the organizations also cite general public interest goals such as promoting understanding of the Government of the United States and the Presidency. Each organization operates under its own charter and may emphasize its support for scholarly programs of the library, museums and public programs, or all aspects of its activities.[5]

Detailed information regarding each of the established supporting organizations is provided in appendix 3.

INSTRUCTIONS TO USERS

All presidential libraries provide instructions to introduce users to the library and its resources and procedures.[6] With the exception of the statement dealing with copyright, which was written by the Office of Presidential Libraries, the libraries have developed their own individual instructions.[7] The Office of Presidential Libraries has reviewed these instructions to ensure their conformity to the National Archives regulations,[8] and to the general policies of the presidential libraries as set down in the Presidential Libraries Manual.[9]

User instructions are generally presented as introductions to the published list of holdings of historical materials. Some libraries, however, have issued instructions on separate sheets. Most libraries give detailed introductory guidance, although others offer only brief explanations. The topics usually brought to the attention of researchers are research application, research room procedures, involvement of archivists, access to materials, types of materials held by the library, finding aids, restrictions, citing historical materials, and copyright provisions.

Research Applications

Persons who desire to use papers and other historical library materials are urged, and by some libraries requested, to write the director of the library before making a trip to the library. In their letter, they should indicate the sources they wish to consult. The library staff can then determine whether there is enough material to make a trip worthwhile and make the proper recommendation to the inquirer. Researchers who visit the library must fill out a research application, a standard form used by all presidential libraries.

While not indispensible as a prerequisite for admission to the library, the researcher is asked to describe the research project, cite his or her occupation and academic background, and note the expected result of research. Upon approval of the research application, the prospective researcher will be issued an identification card.

Research Room Procedures

These procedures are designed to make library use as efficient as possible while ensuring the safety and protection of the papers and other library materials. Researchers may not help themselves to the materials by going directly to the shelves or cabinets that hold them. All research materials are brought to the researcher by a research room attendant. The material must be used at the researcher's assigned location. Researchers are cautioned to use extreme care when examining the papers; to avoid misplacement they use materials from one box or folder at a time. After use, materials must be replaced in the original order. The use of ink or other writing materials that might damage papers is prohibited.

Finding Aids

Access to materials is facilitated by means of finding aids of varying completeness, complexity, and scope. Preliminary inventories, which are modeled after the registers used in the Library of Congress, give the most complete description. There are less detailed lists, which give titles of folders and boxes and list them in the sequence in which they are arranged on the shelves. Each library has additional finding aids to meet specific needs. For instance, the Kennedy Library has a name/subjct index to the open interviews of the oral history collection. The Ford Library has a card file identifying all White House staff employed during the Ford administration, from messengers to senior advisers. The Truman Library has research topic cards for frequently researched topics.

Withdrawn Materials

Documents may have been withdrawn from the files for various reasons. The donor of materials may stipulate in a deed of gift that certain items may be made available to researchers only after the lapse of a specified period of time. Or items may be removed by the library because they need to be repaired, or items may contain security-classified information and therefore not be generally accessible. In each instance in which a document is withdrawn from the files, a standard withdrawal sheet is inserted in its place.

Role of Archivists

All libraries make researchers aware of the important role of the archivists. Although the archivists cannot act as research associates or research assistants, they can on a limited basis provide valuable help and guidance in locating materials, especially when finding aids are not sufficiently detailed or comprehensive.

Restrictions of Use of Materials

Restrictions may be imposed by the donor in his deed of gift, or they may be based on regulations governing the use of security-classified materials. Channels are provided to the researcher to appeal such restrictions.

Mandatory Declassification Review

This is the appeal method for obtaining permission to use security-classified materials. The researcher must fill out the standard mandatory declassification review form, supplying such identifying characteristics as type of document, date it was created, and title and subject covered.

If the document was created by an agency, the library submits the document to the originating agency, which has the authority to make the declassification decision. If the agency declassifies the document, the agency sends copies of the document directly to the researcher. If the agency denies the request for declassification, the researcher may appeal the decision directly to the agency concerned.

If the document was created by the White House, the presidential library submits copies of the document to the agency that has primary subject interest in the document. The agency gives an advisory opinion. The director evaluates the opinion but renders the actual decision. If the director's decision is contrary to the agency's advice, he or she must inform the agency, which may appeal the proposed action of the director. Should the resulting decision deny a researcher's request for materials, the researcher may submit an appeal to the deputy archivist of the United States.

Documents exempted from declassification in whole or in part within the past year may not be resubmitted for declassification until a year has elapsed.

Restrictions by Donors

A researcher may ask for review of donor-imposed restrictions. The researcher must make the request in writing, citing the documents he or she wishes to examine and identifying each document as fully as possible. The library usually acts upon the request within ten days. If the director denies the request, the researcher may submit an appeal to a three-member board of review headed by the deputy archivist of the United States. The appeal to the board of review must be channeled through the director of the library. No review may be obtained for documents considered for review within the past two years or for documents of a collection that has been open fewer than two years. If the donor has reserved the right to decide whether a document is to be open and denies the request, the donor's decision may not be appealed.

Freedom of Information Act (FOIA)

This act covers only a small portion of the holdings of the several presidential libraries since donated historical materials—the bulk of the holdings—are not subject to it. Only federal records are subject to the act. A researcher may submit requests for access to closed federal records by submitting a written request to the director of the library.

The researcher must state that he or she bases the request on the FOIA and describe the desired document as fully as possible. The library, which must consult with the originating agency, is to respond within ten working days. If the library and the consulted agency requires more time, the period may be extended by ten working days. A negative decision may be appealed to the deputy archivist of the United States. If the deputy archivist also denies the researcher's request, he or she must inform the researcher that he or she can now pursue the right of judicial review.

Citations

The libraries stress the importance of citations as devices for identifying and retrieving documents. The forms suggested by the various libraries are similar but not identical. All libraries agree that a citation should consist of as many components as are necessary for identification. For instance, a memo from Charles Murphy to President Truman, sent on December 15, 1950, deposited in the official Truman Files of the Truman Library, has been bibliograhically recorded in this way: Memorandum, Charles Murphy to the

President, December 15, 1950, O F 799, Truman Papers, Truman Library.

Copyright

Copyright is governed by public law 94–553, effective January 1, 1978. The statement provided by the several libraries presents the provisions that are pertinent to the holdings of the presidential libraries: published works that were previously protected by literary property rights under common law now enjoy statutory rights of authorship. These works need not be registered with the Copyright Office to receive protection. They are protected automatically immediately after their creation. Included are not only materials written for publication but also such other items as letters, informal statements, oral history interviews, photographs, maps, motion pictures, and cartoons. Copyright protection extends over the life of an author plus fifty years. Unpublished and copyrighted works created before January 1, 1978, are protected at least until December 1, 1992.

Researchers must obtain permission from the copyright holder to reproduce copyrighted material. Not subject to copyright are documents prepared by officials or employees of the U.S. government. Also considered in the public domain are documents whose owners have transferred the copyright to the United States. Of great importance is the fair use clause, which authorizes a person to use, without having to obtain the copyright holder's permission, small portions of copyrighted materials in support of scholarship and research and not for commercial exploitation.

NOTES

1. National Archives and Records Administration, *Presidential Libraries Manual* (Washington: NARA, April 15, 1985), pp. 2–1 to 2–14.

2. This section is largely based on information supplied by James E. O'Neill, assistant archivist for presidential libraries, Letter to author, November, 13, 1984, accompanied by National Archives and Records Service, "Basic Eligibility Requirements and Office of Personnel Management Registers for Archivists and Archives Technicians" (Processed).

3. National Archives, Office of Presidential Libraries, "Presidential Libraries Supporting Organizations" (Washington, November 1984), p. 1.

4. Ibid.

5. Ibid.

6. This section is based largely on instructions to users developed by the presidential libraries.

7. Judith Koucky, archivist, Office of Presidential Libraries, Letter to author, February 14, 1986.

8. Code of Federal Regulations (Revised as of July 1, 1985), Title 36, chap. II, applicable sections of pts. 1250–60, and pt. 1280.

9. National Archives and Records Administration, *Presidential Libraries Manual.*

5

The Presidential Libraries: Individual Descriptions

With the exception of the Hoover Presidential Library, the arrangement of the libraries in this chapter agrees with the chronological sequence of the presidencies. The Hoover Library follows the Roosevelt and Truman libraries since they were established before the Hoover Library.

FRANKLIN D. ROOSEVELT PRESIDENTIAL LIBRARY

Franklin D. Roosevelt had many interests, which are reflected in his papers, his collection of books, and the other materials he gathered. His personal library consisted of over 15,000 volumes and represents about one-third of the library's current total book collection. He had books on general history, naval history, economics, public affairs, British and American literary classics, and early juveniles. He collected books on ornithology, as well as books and other items that related to his ancestors, the Roosevelts and the Delanos. He acquired prints and stamps. He preserved his private and business correspondence. Moreover, his mother kept everything he wrote.

Roosevelt was aware that he could not provide personally the facilities for accommodating all the materials he had accumulated before and during the presidency. In addition to providing space and care for the papers and books, Roosevelt also had to protect the numerous gifts, many of them valuable and donated by heads of foreign governments. Roosevelt, with his deep sense of history, was convinced that the materials would be of great historical value and provide unique sources for gaining an understanding not only of his presidency but also of the complex social and political fabric of his time.[1]

On December 2, 1938, he sent a memo he labeled "personal and confidential" to a group of people, including several well-known historians, urged them to study the memo, and invited them to a luncheon at which he presented details of his plan. It evoked a generally favorable reaction. He also arranged for a press conference to be held after the luncheon. The reporters were kept uninformed as to the subject but were promised information on a significant historical event. The event was the plan to create a home for his many materials, a depository that would possibly, but not necessarily, be maintained and operated by the government. The plan was acclaimed by most scholars and by citizens in general. There were, however, a few negative voices. H. G. Jones observed that some "comments in editorials and cartoons echoed their somewhat derisive skepticism and looked for such significance as this announcement might have in its obvious relevance to the 1940 presidential election."[2] To put the project on a broad basis, the original group of scholars was enlarged to thirty, all invited by Roosevelt personally.[3]

A few weeks after the plan was released, an operating agency was created, Franklin D. Roosevelt Library, Inc. This agency was authorized to collect funds and build and equip a library at a place of its choice. It could retain control of the library or transfer it to the government. This broad range of possible arrangements would allow the library to come into being and to function even without government sponsorship and support. Such caution did not prove necessary, however. Enabling legislation was quickly adopted. A joint resolution of Congress authorized the archivist of the United States to accept title to the land on which the library was to be built; it also authorized the corporation to build the library on the site and to accept the historical resources as a gift. The resolution further provided that the United Stated would supply the funds necessary for the operation and maintenance of the library.[4]

Funds for the building were obtained from private sources without any difficulty. Several wealthy people guaranteed the amounts needed, and over 28,000 other persons contributed—some very small amounts, some larger suns. Over $400,000 was collected for the building fund.

In his foreward to the sixth edition of *Historical Materials in the Franklin D. Roosevelt Library*, William R. Emerson, the director, observes that Roosevelt had two major purposes in mind for establishing the library: to preserve the records of his administration and to make these records generally accessible as soon as possible.[5] He achieved both purposes.

The first purpose was realized when Roosevelt made sixteen acres of his Hyde Park estate available on which the library could be erected and when the buildings and grounds were turned over to the government on July 4, 1940. The museum facilities were opened on June 30, 1941, and the research section was opened to students and scholars on May 1, 1946.[6] The second purpose was achieved in stages between 1950, when 85 percent of the FDR library was already accessible, and the present time, when less than one-half of 1 percent remains subject to any restriction.

The papers that came from the White House had been assembled during Roosevelt's presidential years in the following files:[7]

Central Files.

Official File, arranged numerically by subject folder.

President's Personal File, arranged numerically by subject folder.

Alphabetical File, arranged alphabetically by name of persons and some subjects.

Confidential File, arranged alphabetically by subject.

Index to Central Files, with an alphabetical card index.

Historical Materials in the Franklin D. Roosevelt Library provides guidance to researchers, who may then need to use the finding aids to the historical materials. The registration book available in the search room gives basic information about each collection, including biographical data on the person who collected the material, a brief description of the papers, and restrictions, if any. The larger collections have more detailed finding aids, generally a shelf list. For frequently used collections, there are card indexes for selected individual documents.

Roosevelt's hope that the library would attract papers of associates and friends has been amply fulfilled. The library now holds over 150 separate collections. Although it has reached maturity, it is still desirous of rounding out its collection and filling gaps. The acquisition policy is designed to meet this continuous effort.

Acquisition Policy

The acquisition policy and the solicitation efforts relate to materials dealing with four categories:[8]

1. Major figures of the Roosevelt administration and President and Mrs. Roosevelt's major acquaintances.
2. Similar figures of secondary importance.
3. President Roosevelt's family.
4. History of the U.S. Navy, Dutchess County and the Hudson Valley region, and the Dutch immigration and settlement in the American colonies.

The efforts to obtain materials vary. Every reasonable effort is made to obtain materials for category 1. Materials for category 2 are solicited routinely but not exigently; and if materials are proffered, the director may find reasons for suggesting that they be deposited elsewhere. An item might be accepted if refusal would becloud the relationship with the prospective donor. For category 3, the library attempts to get only those that are likely to be significant in documenting President or Mrs. Roosevelt's career; however, family materials not meeting these specifications may be accepted if refusal might have an adverse effect on the relationship with the family. And for category 4, the underlying consideration is to augment the collection of materials assembled by Franklin D. Roosevelt in the hope that the additional materials will contribute to the development of a center of local as well as national history. With regard to these materials, cooperation with other local and regional historical agencies is advised, and prospective donations may be channeled to alternate depositories. "In all such approaches Library staff should remember that they speak in the interests of the archival and historical communities, not those of this Library alone."[9]

With regard to books, completeness is not an aim. Books are viewed mainly as resource materials for the staff in supporting research inquiries. First priority is given to building a comprehensive collection of major books and other printed material on the lives and careers of President and Mrs. Roosevelt and then to forming a less comprehensive collection of items dealing with their principal political and social acquaintances and items dealing with the President's and Mrs. Roosevelt's ideals, causes, and concerns.

The second category embraces reference works, such as *Who's Who in America*, biographical indexes, and others.

The third category, with highly selective purchasing, covers secondary works of lesser weight, of real but peripheral interest on the themes and works in fields in which FDR was an active collector.

In addition to nearly 16 million pages of personal papers and nearly 45,000 books and over 32,000 serials, there are over eighty transcripts of oral histories, of which all but fourteen are Eleanor Roosevelt's transcripts.[10]

Audiovisual Collection

This collection is extensive and covers a great many aspects of Roosevelt's political and private life.[11]

The film collection covering the period from 1912 to the present consists of items donated by Franklin D. Roosevelt, his wife, and other members of the family, as well as by other individuals and by organizations. In recent years, the library has received videocassette tapes of television programs about the Roosevelts.

About 85 percent of the films are black and white; only 15 percent are in color. All 35 mm nitrate films have been converted to safety stock to meet the requirements of the library's preservation program.

The core of the collection of films dealing with Franklin D. Roosevelt consists of newsreels of such companies as Pathe, Hearst, and Movietone News. They depict activities from the time of the 1932 campaign until his death. Some Roosevelt films in color were produced by government agencies. In this group are films covering the visit of King George VI of England, wartime inspection trips, and overseas conferences, including the Yalta Conference.

Amateur films in the collection give informal glimpses of Roosevelt. We see him in his office at Warm Springs, on an Erie Canal barge trip, sailing on the yacht *Sequoia*, and visiting with Winston Churchill and the duke of Windsor at Hyde Park.

The still pictures, now numbering over 130,000, are distributed among the General Collection, which holds nearly half the total and about fifteen other collections of varying size. In addition, there are a number of small collections formed from photographs included with gifts of manuscripts. The collection contains photographs taken by the Roosevelts, including FDR, and friends, as well as commercial photographers. Some photographs go back to the daguerreotype period.

The photographs depict many scenes: FDR, Eleanor, and members of the family and associates; scenes from the war and the homefront; pictures of libraries and archives; and prints illustrating the history of the U.S. Navy from the Revolutionary War to World War II.

The Building

It comprises 72,328 square feet. The original cost was $376,000.

The building, whose architectural style was inspired by old Hudson Valley farmhouses, was enlarged by two wings dedicated in honor of Eleanor Roosevelt on May 3, 1972.[12] One wing contains enlarged research facilities. The other includes an exhibition gallery devoted to Mrs. Roosevelt's life and an auditorium where part of the president's naval collection is displayed.

The museum has extensive displays on FDR's life and career, photographs, objects he used personally and objects he received as gifts, many family items, letters, speeches, important documents of general interest, such as the president's statement on the significance of the Social Security bill when he signed it on August 14, 1935, and the message to Congress of December 8, 1941, calling for a declaration of war on Japan. It also contains the letter of Albert Einstein instrumental in the development of the atomic bomb.

Use of the Library

The library makes its holdings available to any person pursuing a legitimate study requiring the use of its unique resources. In 1985 there were approximately 195,000 museum visitors and over 1,000 researcher vists.

Budget

The budget figures for fiscal year 1983 were $561,000; for 1984, $566,000; and for 1985, $569,000. In each year, personnel expenditures claimed over 90 percent of the total budget. The trust fund provides an income of $175,000 annually and is usually used to support income-producing activities serving the public.

Personnel

The professional staff consists of sixteen persons (nine archivists, three librarians, and four other professionals). There also are eight technical assistants and a varying number of maintenance and security staff.

Publications

The library has issued several books and pamphlets, among them William J. Stewart, compiler, *The Era of Franklin D. Roosevelt, A Selected Bibliography of Periodical, Essay and Dissertation Literature, 1945–1971* (1974); James Whitehead, *The Museum of the Franklin D. Roosevelt Library* (1974); and Edgar B. Nixon, compiler, *Franklin D. Roosevelt and Conservation, 1911–1945* 2 vols. (1957). Also available from the library are rolls of microfilm: *Press Conferences of Franklin D. Roosevelt, 1933–45*; *A Comprehensive Index to the Press Conferences*; *Roosevelt-Churchill Messages*; *Papers of Henry A. Wallace as Vice-President 1941–44*; *The Diary of Adolf A. Berle.*

HARRY S. TRUMAN PRESIDENTIAL LIBRARY

The Harry S. Truman Library is the first presidential library established in accordance with the Presidential Libraries Act of 1955.[13] The Roosevelt Library was the first federally administered and supported library; however, the joint resolution creating it applied only to the Roosevelt Library.[14]

The Harry S. Truman Library was built by Harry S. Truman Library, Inc., with funds contributed by some 17,000 people. The cost of the library without the land, donated by the city of Independence, Missouri, was $1,750,000. The original structure, built of Indiana sandstone, was enlarged by two additions, the first in 1968 and the second in 1980, at a cost of $310,000 and $2,800,000, respectively. The library building, a one-story full basement structure, "is roughly circular in configuration with a circumference measuring approximately 1,000 feet and with a total floor space of nearly 100,000 square feet.... The building surrounds a courtyard where President Truman [and his wife are] buried."[15]

The building and the Presidential papers were transferred to the federal government at a dedication ceremony held on July 6, 1957.

The building houses papers and other kinds of materials relating to President Truman's public and private life.

Of a total collection consisting of about 13,200,000 manuscript materials, the Truman papers number about 7,488,000 pages, of which about 6,538,000 were produced during the presidency, 220,000 before, and 730,000 after the presidency. The presidential papers include the office files of individual members of Truman's White House staff and files maintained by the White House staff offices.

The major portion of Truman's White House files consists of the President's Secretary's Files (PSF) and the White House Central

Files. The PSF contain material the president wished to retain under his control because of its confidential nature.

The White House Central Files served as the central files for the entire White House staff. They were broken down into three principal groups: the Official File, the President's Personal File, and the General File.[16]

Items of a sensitive nature are segregated from the principal series and assigned to the Confidential File. Also separated from the principal series are items containing information on precedents. They are assigned to the Permanent File.

In addition to the Truman papers, the library has custody of more than 385 manuscript collections from persons associated with Truman in an official or personal capacity. The library continues in its efforts to build up these resources and welcomes additional collections from persons who held office in Truman's administration from 1945 to 1953 and from friends and other persons otherwise associated with him.

The Truman Library further holds some federal records related to Truman's activities and interests, mainly records of federal commissions and committees appointed by Truman during his presidency.

The audiovisual collection consists of still pictures, motion pictures, videotapes, audiotapes, and audio discs in the quantities noted in table 2.

The still pictures cover Truman's career, with emphasis on the presidency. The collection also has photographs of Truman's personal and political associates. The sound recordings contain reproductions of many of Truman's addresses and informal remarks.

The motion picture collection represents mainly Truman and his administration. The films cover both the presidential and postpresidential periods. The films come from commercial sources and private donors.[17]

Books and Periodicals

The book collection consists of about 44,800 items. The periodicals collection numbers nearly 75,000 items. Subjects emphasized are Truman's public career, the careers of political and personal associates, and U.S. history from 1945 to 1953. The library also collects theses and dissertations written about Truman and his administration. The library's collection of printed books includes nearly 3,000 microfilm copies of printed materials.

The library has a microfilm collection consisting of materials from over thirty primary sources.[18] The originals are held by other depositories and individuals. The papers are mostly from Truman administrative officials and records of agencies from the Truman administration. The entry for each item includes the name of the individual or organization whose papers are filmed, the name of the depository holding the paper, the National Union Catalog of Manuscript Collection (NUMC) identification number, and the number of reels.

In addition, the library has microfilm copies of the papers of nineteen former presidents held by the Library of Congress. (In all, the Library of Congress holds the bulk of the papers of twenty-three presidents.) The Truman Library also has microfilm copies of the Adams family papers, which are deposited in the Massachusetts Historical Society.[19]

In 1961, the library established the Oral History Project.[20] Since staff and funds have been limited, subjects of particular interest to students of the Truman period have been given preference. Special attention has been given to Truman's presenatorial career, the work of the White House staff during his administration, and U.S. foreign policy, mainly during the years 1945 through 1952. Special interview projects were conducted in 1964 and in 1970–1971. They dealt largely with foreign aid programs. In all, the interview collection covers over 44,000 pages.

Arrangement of Materials

In arranging the papers, the original file order has been maintained. The White House Central Files were arranged by the file room staff and the others by the White House staff while the president was in office.

Books are classified in accordance with the Library of Congress scheme. Periodicals are arranged alphabetically by title and within titles chronologically. Photographs and other audiovisual items are filed by accession number.

Museum Collection

This collection contains about 21,000 items. The objects illustrate significant aspects of Truman's career and the history of the United States during the period 1945 to 1953.[21]

Upon entering the lobby, visitors face the mural *Independence and the Opening of the West*, by Thomas Hart Benton. Displayed in the east foyer are gifts to President Truman from foreign countries. The exhibit "That Most American of Games" shows buttons, cards, ballots, posters, and other memorabilia pertaining to presidential campaigns and inaugurations from 1828 to 1977. Among the other permanent exhibits are a reproduction of the president's White House office as it appeared during the Truman administration.

The president's World War I service is documented in the Thirty-fifth Division Room. The 1948 campaign is concentrated in the 1948 Campaign Room. Among other displays highlighted are those concerning the Potsdam Conference, the dropping of the first atomic bomb, the end of World War II, and the Korean War. Other displayed items include the piano the president liked to play while in the White House, the presidential limousine, and a mantle from the state dining room.

There are frequent showings of films and programs in the museum's auditorium.

Staff

The staff consists of eighteen professional members (nine archivists, two librarians, seven museum and other professional staff persons) and twenty-two nonprofessional employees (three technical assistants, eight clerks, five buildings and ground personnel, and six security personnel).

Use

In 1985 the Truman Library was visited by 188,552 museum vistors. There were in addition 1,206 research visits.

Budget

The appropriated funds for 1983 were $660,000; for 1984 $719,000; and for 1985 $738,000. The appropriated sums have been augmented by museum admission fees and profits from sales items, including profits from sales of materials from the audiovisual collection, and fees for electrostatic copies of papers.

Harry S. Truman Library Institute

This institute, a nonprofit corporation, was organized in 1957 to promote the library's growth and development.[22] The institute encourages the acquisition of research materials; it provides financial assistance to scholars; it sponsors scholarly conferences; and it fosters research based on the library's holdings. While emphasizing the promotion of research dealing with the Truman administration, the institute is also designed to further an understanding of the nature and functions of the U.S. government. The institute pursues its work in cooperation with historical and educational agencies.

Each year the institute awards grants-in-aid of up to $1,000 to individuals studying the Truman administration. And each year, one scholar who works on an advanced project may receive the Tom L. Evans Research Grant of $10,000. In odd-numbered years, the institute awards a $20,000 senior research fellowship to a scholar who prepares a book-length publication.

HERBERT HOOVER PRESIDENTIAL LIBRARY

The Herbert Hoover Presidential Library is located at West Branch, Iowa, Hoover's birthplace. The library is on the grounds of the 187-acre Herbert Hoover National Historical Site, which is administered by the National Park Service of the Department of the Interior. Other buildings and facilities on the site are Hoover's birthplace cottage, his father's blacksmith shop, the Friends' meeting house, the first West Branch school, and the Hoover grave site.[23]

The library building was formally dedicated on August 10, 1962, Hoover's eighty-eighth birthday. On August 10, 1964, Hoover's ninetieth birthday, the birthplace, library, and grounds were deeded to the federal government. In March 1966, the building was opened to research workers. Before this date, only the museum objects could be viewed by the visitors. The library building is 27,000 square feet in size. The building was enlarged by two additions (in 1971 and in 1973–1974). The original building was financed by the Hoover Birthplace Foundation (whose name was changed in 1972 to Hoover Presidential Library Association); the cost for the additions was borne by the federal government.

Regarding building projects and costs, Robert Wood, the director of the Library, observes: "There were four building projects involved in the construction of the Library. The first two, which were funded by the Herbert Hoover Birthplace Foundation, cost about $2,000,000. This is an estimate. This does not include 180 acres of land and the NHS building. I do not have the actual figures. The two additions added by the government were $623,860,690 in 1970–71 and $352,815,900 in 1973–74."[24]

Before the presidential library was built, the papers of Herbert Hoover were in the Hoover Institution, Stanford University. With the exception of the papers dealing with Hoover's World War I relief activities (1918–1923), the papers were moved to West Branch in 1962. The library also obtained copies of major documents relating to World War I relief and reconstruction.[25] After Hoover's death in

1964, materials from his office in the Waldorf Astoria Towers were also sent to West Branch.

The papers cover Hoover's whole life span. Produced before the presidency were 731,400 pages; during the presidency, 898,400 pages; and after the presidency, 680,400 pages. Also included are papers from Hoover's wife, Lou Henry Hoover. These papers, still unprocessed, cover 260,000 pages. Further there are 402,000 pages of papers from presidential advisers and 16,800 from members of the cabinet in office during the presidency. The Hoover special collections number 394,200 pages, and the general accessions, covering 121 collections, number 3,357,062 pages.

To facilitate research, the papers of Herbert Hoover have been divided chronologically into five subgroups, each covering a distinct period of his life. In addition to the chronologically arranged items, there are eight special collections spanning nearly all of Hoover's career.[26]

With regard to the arrangement of the papers, the library prefers to follow the original scheme whenever it is practical from a reference point of view. The White House Central Files arrangement was modified when Hoover considered this desirable for his research needs before he donated the materials to the government.

Books and Periodicals

The library has a collection of over 24,000 books relating largely to the period 1874–1964. The library also has a collection of nearly 27,000 periodicals. Books and periodicals are classified in accordance with the Library of Congress classification scheme.

Audiovisual Materials

The collection has various types of audiovisual materials. Still photographs, in excess of 32,000, cover a wide array of subjects: the ancestry of the Hoover family; boyhood and student life; famine relief after World Wars I and II; construction of the Hoover Dam; activities at the Hoover Presidential Library; photographs from various manuscript collections; and photographs of rooms, furniture, and grounds of the White House.

Cards for the photographs are filed in a photo catalog consisting of cards bearing a reduced-size photograph and description of the item. The cards are filed by name, subject, and date.

The motion picture collection consists of over 151,000 feet of 16 mm movies. The collection is divided into professional and Hoover family home film. The library has a list of titles, descriptions, and copyright owners.

Sound recordings include videotapes, audiotapes, and audio discs. The materials date from Herbert Hoover's speech to the American Steel Institute in 1927 to Julie Nixon Eisenhower's address on the occasion of Hoover's ninety-eighth birthday in 1972. Also recorded is Hoover's last public address on August 10, 1962, at the dedication of the Hoover Library. The library has a chronological list of the tapes available.

The Oral History Program, established in 1966, is privately funded. The interviews, well over 300, cover nearly 11,000 pages. A composite card index facilitates the use of these materials.

To deepen and to extend the scope of the collection, the library has assembled microfilms of related historical source materials that are held by other depositories or individuals. In each instance, the following information is provided: name of the individual or organization represented, inclusive date of the filmed materials, name of the depository holding the original, and number of reels in the group.[27]

The library has no plans to microfilm its own collection.

Museum Services

The museum provides public services through exhibits and educational programs. The exhibits contain documents, photographs, and memorabilia that illustrate Hoover's life from 1874 to 1974. The exhibits show Hoover as a many-sided, versatile, public-minded person whose life is distinguished by numerous accomplishments, including relief administrator during both world wars, secretary of commerce, and president. The displays are arranged in chronological order.

The museum offers educational programs and shows films on a regular schedule during the summer and, upon request, to groups during the rest of the year. The staff is available for reference service. Educational materials may be examined on the premises or may be ordered by mail. The Outreach Program brings slides to groups within the region.

The Hoover Library offers conferences and seminars. Examples of typical significant conferences are "Herbert Hoover's Social Philosophy and Contemporary America," April 13–14, 1982, and "The Problems of Lasting Peace," November 1–2, 1983.

Use of Library

In fiscal year 1985, the Hoover Library and Museum was visited by 50,310 persons. The admission figure comprises 32,171 paid and 18,139 free admissions. There were in addition 604 researcher visits.

The manuscript collections are freely accessible to anyone with an academic purpose. Researchers need not be academics.

Staff

The professional staff consists of seven archivists and one curator. One archivist serves as a part-time librarian. The nonprofessional staff numbers nine persons, with these specializations: archives technician, museum technician, library technician, exhibit specialist, sales desk clerk, administrative officer, and budget assistant.

Budget

Appropriated funds for the operating budget years for fiscal year 1983 were $516,000; for fiscal year 1984, $493,000; and for fiscal year 1985, $477,000.

DWIGHT D. EISENHOWER PRESIDENTIAL LIBRARY

The Eisenhower Presidential Library complex at Abilene, Kansas, also called Eisenhower Center, consists of five separate buildings on a land area of 13.4 acres: the library building, a separate museum building, the family home, the place of meditation, and the visitors' center.

The Dwight D. Eisenhower Library was dedicated on May 1, 1962; it was opened to the public in 1966. The museum was dedicated on Veterans' Day in 1954. The library occupies 55,000 square feet and the museum 25,000 square feet.

The library cost $1.8 million and the museum $400,000. The Eisenhower Museum was constructed by the Eisenhower Foundation with funds raised through public subscriptions and gifts. The Eisenhower Library was built with contributions from friends of the former president. The funds were administered by the Eisenhower Presidential Library Commission. In 1966, the Eisenhower Library and the Eisenhower Museum were deeded to the United States.

The Eisenhower Library is described as a "rectangular structure, two stories in height, of modern, architectural design . . . simple exterior of the building is Kansas limestone and provides a contrast to the extensive use of marble inside the building."[28]

Although there is a separate museum building, there are also exhibit areas in the library intended to complement the exhibits in the museum. The museum, located across the street from the library, was constructed of Kansas limestone. In the lobby are murals illustrating significant elements of Eisenhower's career from childhood through the presidency. Exhibits in the separate wings of the museum show items associated with the president and his family up to and including the presidency and the postpresidential years.

The materials in the Eisenhower Library and the Eisenhower Museum reflect the diverse interests of Dwight D. Eisenhower, who had several distinct careers: soldier, president for two terms, university president, and elder statesman whose advice was solicited by members of both political parties.[29]

The bulk of the Eisenhower papers, about 10 million pages, was produced during the presidency; about 4.6 million pages were produced before the presidency and about 4 million after the presidency. About 700,000 pages of papers are from the presidential family, about 3,680,000 from presidential advisers, and about 700,000 from members of the cabinet in office during the presidency. About 2.8 million pages are from World War II, and 1,660,000 pages represent miscellaneous collections.

The presidential papers of greatest importance are contained in the president's office files, which were maintained by Ann Whitman, Eisenhower's personal secretary. They are frequently designated as the Ann Whitman File.[30] This collection of about 274,000 pages includes Eisenhower's correspondence with heads of state, government officials, friends, and associates; it also includes memoranda, press releases, reports, and other communications dealing with domestic and foreign policies of the Eisenhower administration.

At the start of the Eisenhower administration, Ann Whitman established the filing system for the president's office files and was responsible for the files until Eisenhower left office. The Eisenhower Library has preserved the files in the arrangement she devised, although several files have been renamed to reflect their contents more accurately. At Eisenhower's request, these papers were shipped to Gettysburg at the close of his administration. He used them in the preparation of his memoirs, *The White House Years*. After his death in 1969, the papers were transferred to the Eisenhower Library. Six series, about 50 percent, became available for research in 1975; the twelve remaining series became available by March 1983. Portions of these papers are closed because of donor restrictions or government regulations.

The president's own files are also known as the Dwight D. Eisenhower papers. The White House Central Files are considered the Dwight D. Eisenhower Records.

The White House Central Files (1953–1961) represent the largest collection in the Library and consist of about 6.5 million pages. The Central Files contain papers relating to all of the major foreign and domestic issues and to the political events of the Eisenhower administration. Approximately 2.2 million pages dealing with the more significant aspects of the administration have already been processed. The segments not yet processed are largely of little historical value. Among them are message requests from organizations, requests for photographs, and birthday congratulations.[31]

Finding Aids

The finding aids are of varying detail and sophistication.[32] Fullest description is given in the Preliminary Inventory modeled on registers used by the Library of Congress. The shelf list is less detailed. It shows the box-by-box and folder-by-folder organization of materials. Finally, a mere registration statement is represented by the letter R. Another helpful finding aid is the "Quarterly List of Declassified Documents," which includes all documents that have been declassified in the course of the quarter as a result of mandatory review requests.

Information on recent accessions, collection openings, and recently declassified materials can be found in *Prologue: The Journal of the National Archives*.[33] The Eisenhower Foundation provides similar information in *Overview*, its newsletter.

Books and Periodicals

A book collection of about 22,000 titles relates mostly to the period during which Eisenhower lived. It contains a mixture of presidential reading materials and gifts from friends and admirers. The library also has acquired reference books and other titles to facilitate the work of staff and research workers. Included in the book collection are about 800 reels of microfilmed theses and dissertations. The books are classified in accordance with the Library of Congress scheme. The library holds about 34,000 serials. Noteworthy is the collection of periodical materials by or about Eisenhower; they are part of the Vertical File holdings.

Audiovisual Holdings

These holdings consist of 188,284 still pictures, 576 motion picture films (501 of which are 16 mm type), 19 videotapes, and approximately 1,100 audiotapes and discs.[34] Table 2 gives the data for films in feet and for tapes and discs in hours. The audiovisual collection has been formed by contributions from private individuals, organizations, and governmental agencies.

Most photographic materials were received as part of the manuscript collections; they are identified by name of donor. Within individual collections, photographs are arranged chronologically.

In addition to about 600,000 feet of original motion picture film, the collection has some 365,000 feet of duplicate copies for research use. Most of the films cover the presidential years and are donations by the Columbia Broadcasting System. The collection also has some documentary films relating to World War II, including the film version of Eisenhower's book, *Crusade in Europe*.

The audiotapes and discs cover the period 1940 to the late 1960s. These materials, mainly produced by the Army Signal Corps, illustrate primarily President Eisenhower's roles in ceremonial occasions, national addresses, and press conferences. All audiovisual materials except photographs are arranged by accession number, which is based on the date accessioned. To expedite retrieval, cross-references have been provided in the form of alphabetical, chronological, geographical, and numerical categories.

Oral History

The oral history collection consists of two main components: transcripts of interviews conducted by the Eisenhower Library and transcripts of interviews obtained by agreement with Columbia University.[35] The library's own program began in 1963 and continues to the present time. The cooperation with Columbia University was initiated in 1960 and lasted until 1973. In addition to these two main components, the library holds fifty-five transcripts from the Regional Oral History Office of the Bancroft Library of the University of California at Berkeley, as well as a number of interviews from various other institutions. Each entry gives the source of the interview, the date, and the number of pages.

Museum Services

The museum possesses over 28,000 objects.[36] It is particularly rich in military-related materials. They are from several historical periods, but World War II is most heavily represented. The collection contains numerous awards, orders, medals, and other symbols of distinction bestowed on Dwight D. Eisenhower. The Britt Brown Small Arms Collection, distinguished for its samples of most small arms used during World War II, includes many samples of the accoutrements used with the weapons and the operating instructions and operating manuals issued for the weapons. Also rare is an allied military currency collection. Further, there are small numismatic and philatelic collections. Visitors have shown great interest in the political cartoon collection and the collection of campaign objects.

The museum houses many art objects, some of them gifts to Dwight D. Eisenhower during World War II and the White House years. All kinds of art forms are represented, among them portraits, landscapes, American primitives, prints from as early as the eighteenth century, and sculpture. Also part of the collection are various types of oriental art, such as scrolls and cloisonné.

The museum objects are cataloged in accordance with the museum registration methods proposed by the American Association of Museums. Subject files are based on and developed through the program described in *Nomenclature for Museum Cataloging* by Robert G. Chenhall.[37]

Staff

The professional staff consists of eight archivists, one of whom serves as a half-time librarian, and seven other professional staff members, four of whom are assigned to the museum. The nonprofessional staff consists of five archives technicians, four clerks, and four others with various responsibilities.

Use

In fiscal year 1985, there were about 115,000 museum visitors and 748 researcher visits.

Budget

The appropriated funds were $600,000 for 1983, $656,000 for 1984, and $708,000 for 1985. One-half percent is spent on solicitation, travel, conferences, and so on.

Publication

The Dwight D. Eisenhower Library has published *Dwight D. Eisenhower: A Selected Bibliography of Periodical and Dissertation Literature* (1981).

Conferences

Periodically, conferences reflecting the many concerns of Dwight D. Eisenhower have been held. In March 1969 there was a conference on the history of the American West. In addition to the presentation of the papers, the conference initiated a month-long art show. Also in 1969, two other conferences, one in March and one in April, were held to help Kansas museums develop staffs. The meetings were heavily attended and resulted in the formation of the Kansas Museum Association with a member of the Eisenhower Library as its first president.

From September 25 to 27, 1980, there was a conference on America in the 1950s. One session dealt with "The Red Scare and Blacklisting" with John H. Faulk, a victim, as keynote speaker. Other sessions dealt with "The Hot and Cold War" and with "Civil Rights in the 1950's."

A conference held October 11–15, 1982, focused on "Leadership in NATO: Past and Present" with such outstanding participants as Bernard W. Rogers, supreme allied commander in Europe, and Generals Louis Norstadt and Lyman L. Lemnitzer, SHAPE (Supreme Headquarters Allied Powers Europe [NATO]) commanders 1956–1963 and 1963–1969, respectively.

"The American Dream," a conference that took place on April 20 and 21, 1983, reflected on such topics as "Rags to Riches: American Success Stories"; "Sharing the Dream"; "Selling the American Dream"; "Turning Out the Dream—Utopias"; and "Other Anti-Establishment Movements."

JOHN F. KENNEDY PRESIDENTIAL LIBRARY

The John F. Kennedy Library building at Boston harbor was dedicated October 20, 1979. Dan H. Fenn, the library's director, describes the circumstances that led to the structure's being built in Boston rather than in Cambridge as President Kennedy had envisioned.[38] On his last visit to Boston in October 1963, Kennedy considered several sites. The site he preferred was on the Charles River across the street from Harvard's undergraduate houses. Kennedy had reason to believe that this site could be obtained, since initially

it was generally favored and obstacles involving the necessary re-
location of the Metropolitan Boston Transit Authority yards had
been overcome. However, a number of people who lived near the
projected library formed an opposition group. To avoid protracted
controversy and above all to be able to have the library and museum
facilities in one building, the John F. Kennedy Library Corporation
abandoned the plan for a building in Cambridge. The corporation
accepted the offer of the University of Massachusetts to build the
library in Boston on the Columbia Point campus.

The structure is 110 feet high and near the water's edge. The total
area covered by the building is 115,000 square feet.

Funds for the building have come from private sources. Over $18
million have been collected from over 30,000 people, including school
children.

Papers

The National Archives and Records Service of the General Services Administration assumed responsibility for organizing the papers after Kennedy's death. In 1965, the executors of John F.
Kennedy's estate transferred the papers and other materials to the
library.[39] In 1966 the materials were moved to the new Federal
Records Center in Waltham, Massachusetts, the temporary location
of the library. It was expected that the facilities in Waltham would
be needed for only a short time and that the library would soon have
its own quarters, but the library in Boston was not ready for occupation until 1979.

The library staff began to process the papers and also, to the extent
that time permitted, to offer reference service in its temporary quarters. When the library moved into its building at Columbia Point,
most of the substantive papers had been processed.

The library holds the papers of President John F. Kennedy, his
brother Robert F. Kennedy, and collections of other individuals and
organizations and some records of government agencies. The library
also has audiovisual holdings and oral history interviews and possesses museum objects of various kinds.

The papers of John F. Kennedy represent the core of the library's
collections of papers. The Kennedy papers consist of the following
units:[40]

1. Personal papers (20 linear feet, five reels of microfilm). They are
   composed of papers that had been previously scattered through
   various collections and were brought together for more convenience
   in research. They include materials on early years, Harvard records
   and Harvard notebooks, accounts and bills, and doodles.

2. Prepresidential papers, 1947–1960 (430 linear feet). These are the official files of John F. Kennedy's legislative career. They consist of the House of Representatives Files (1947–1952) and the Senate Files (1953–1960). Within this unit are the files covering the several campaigns, as well as the Transition Files. Most of these files are open. Among the few closed files are those containing service academy applications and appointments.

3. Presidential papers, 1961–1963 (3454 linear feet). They consist of the following:

President's Office Files: The files of the president maintained by his secretary, Evelyn Lincoln.

National Security Files: The working files of the assistant to the president for national security affairs.

White House Central Files: Composed of the Subject File, Name File, Chronological File, and Security Classified File (containing national security classified material withdrawn from the Subject Files by the White House Central File Office.)

White House Social Files.

Bureau of the Budget Bill Reports: Consists of memorials to the president from the assistant director of the Bureau of the Budget for Legislative Reference; recommendations of agency heads to the Bureau of the Budget; and copies of bills, acts, and committee reports.

Miscellaneous Presidential Files: Include congratulations, greetings, oversized materials from the White House Central Files, and public opinion mail.

White House Staff Files: Materials needed by White House staff members for carrying out their day-to-day work.

Papers of Postassassination period, 1963–1974 (1570 linear feet): Articles, sermons, condolences, testimonies, music, essays, poetry, and resolutions of foreign governments in response to Kennedy's assassination.

Collections of personal and organization papers:[41] Embraces not only papers of people who were friends or associates of John F. and Robert F. Kennedy but also of others who could contribute to an understanding of the Kennedy era. Also included are papers from foundations and organizations such as the Democratic National Committee. The collections are listed alphabetically under the name of the individual or organization except for two collections, composed of small items within their respective subject files: "Historical Manuscripts and Autographs" and "Literary Manuscript Collections."

John F. Kennedy's special interest in the life and works of Ernest Hemingway is reflected in the Ernest Hemingway Collection, which contains draft manuscripts of books, correspondence, and monographs. Access to these papers—over 170 collections—is subject to the conditions set by the donor.

Records

A number of government agencies have deposited official records with a bearing on the Kennedy administration.[42] Some are on paper and some on microfilm. Some are closed and can be inspected only on authorization of the originating agency.

Audiovisual Collection

The audiovisual materials have come from various sources.[43] The bulk of the collection is White House originated; however, contributions have also been made by various government agencies, private organizations, and private individuals.

Of the total group of still pictures (135,000), about 30,000 were made by White House photographers. Most are of public functions. Also included are pictures of the president on vacation with his family. Other donors of photographs are various government agencies, which have taken pictures of visits to installations. Among the other donors are newspapers, magazines, wire press agencies, and individuals, many from foreign countries who donated snapshots and many taken while the president traveled through the donor's country.

The core of the sound recordings collection consists of tapes of presidential addresses and remarks recorded by the White House Communication Agency between 1961 and 1963. Recordings donated by private organizations reach back to 1944, but the bulk covers the years 1952 through 1964. They include the entire Democratic conventions of 1956 and 1960 and other political speeches and advertisements. A number of individuals have donated tapes and discs, many of them memorials to the president, songs, poetry, and music.

Some films have been donated by the major television networks and government organizations, but the bulk of the collection was supplied by White House photographers and individuals. A number of private organizations, such as Guggenheim Productions and the Democratic National Committee, have supplied large quantities of film footage.

The motion pictures cover a wide range of activities: trips, meetings, ceremonial occasions, political campaigns, interviews, addresses, and official functions of specific agencies. White House photographers who took the pictures of official activities were also permitted to film the president when on leisure—for instance, on weekends at Hyannisport and Palm Beach. Many of the films will be unavailable until preservation copies have been made.

Cartoons

Most of the cartoons highlight events in Kennedy's family and his career. Some are reactions to his assassination. Others go back to 1876 and illustrate the issues of international, national, and local concerns.

Oral History Interviews

The oral history program was begun in 1964.[44] By the end of 1982, 1,176 interviews had been conducted, and 681 of these were open to researchers. Interviews were given by a wide variety of people, prominent figures as well as less well-known ones. The interviews are intended to represent the individual's considered judgment, truly expressed. They are not meant to be monuments to the president. To deepen an understanding of Robert F. Kennedy's personality and work, the interview program included interviews with Robert F. Kennedy as its subject.

Books and Other Printed Material

The Kennedy Library covers a broad range of materials relating to the life and career of President Kennedy.[45] The library administration has endeavored to build up a definitive body of Kennedy-related literature and to make the library the center for Kennedy studies. The types of materials collected should accomplish this objective. The categories encompass the following:

Books written by President Kennedy (if several printings have been made, all will be acquired).

Books by and about members of the family.

Studies pertaining to the Kennedy administration and selected published writings of Kennedy's associates. An example is Stewart Udall's The *Quiet Crisis*, with an introduction by John F. Kennedy.

Studies relating to the presidency.

Books based in part or fully on the library's resources.

Dissertations, theses, and research papers dealing with aspects of John F. Kennedy's career.

Reference books such as biographical and bibliographical works, encyclopedias, and guides.

Special collections such as the Hemingway collection, which is augmented by criticisms and evaluations that may have appeared in
the book and periodical literature. The Hemingway collection includes the author's work in foreign editions.

The books have been cataloged in accordance with the Library of
Congress classification. In order to facilitate retrieval, the Kennedy
Library staff has augmented the subject heading list by over 275
Kennedy-oriented headings. Readers can discover highlights of the
Kennedy administration by means of headings such as the following:
"Kennedy, John Fitzgerald—For. Rel.—Cuba, October, 1962."[46]

Periodical literature is acquired to the extent that it has a bearing
on John F. Kennedy's life and career. The library maintains a file
of rare and noteworthy articles, papers, and related materials that
allow in-depth coverage of personalities and events of the Kennedy
era. Also designed to increase the research potential of the library
are clippings from many sources (assembled in over 400 scrapbooks)
and over 200 volumes of clippings from Boston newspapers.

Acquisition Policy

The papers of John F. Kennedy represent the core of the collection.
The library tries to acquire first-person items associated with these
papers—for instance, signature copies of outgoing correspondence
that may have gone astray. Efforts are also made to acquire papers
of Kennedy's immediate family, close personal friends, and his principal political and governmental associates. Definitive lifetime papers are sought in particular of John F. Kennedy's father, his
brothers Robert and Edward, and also of other members of the family, especially if they were engaged in public service.

Lifetime papers of presidential employees and principal White
House staff members are also sought, as are papers from others who
may have had a distinguished public service career and whose files
would be contributory to the pursuit of future scholarship. At times
papers on specific issues may be sought from persons who might
shed light on such issues.[47]

To provide up-to-date information about acquisitions and newly
opened collections or parts of collections, the library issues lists from
time to time.[48]

Museum Services

The museum is arranged in such a way that visitors pass through
a central, circular-shaped area that contains the presidential desk

and a series of exhibits, each illustrating a different set of presidential functions (for instance, a presidential day or a presidential press conference). The exhibits are intended to serve as background for special tours for students and others. Some themes for tours are the "Responsiblities of a Cabinet Officer" and "Development of a Legislative Initiative and Campaigning." Other exhibits stress the president's roots, starting with Irish immigration in 1840.

The museum staff, in addition to accessioning and cataloging the museum objects and to preparing, arranging, and displaying the exhibits within the building, also has extramural obligations. The staff initiates, participates in, and contributes to special exhibits at local schools, colleges, museums, and other cultural organizations.[49]

The library has a strong multifaceted educational program.[50] It employs many forms and formats using the device most likely to be effective for a particular audience, which may be an elementary school class, a group of graduate students, or a mixed group drawn from the general public. The library has offered seminars and conferences for community groups. The topics chosen often can be supported by materials in the collection. Favorite topics have been government, politics, the presidency, the career and life of John F. Kennedy. The library has conducted various workshops, such as one for community college teachers from four states, and summer workshops for teachers in the Boston school system to help them improve their teaching of politics and government.

The Kennedy Assassinations

There has been wide interest in the circumstances surrounding the tragic death of John F. Kennedy and his brother, Robert. To respond to this interest, the library has assembled a collection of materials and has recorded the items in a bibliography entitled *Kennedy Assassinations*. The pamphlet lists all items dealing with John F. Kennedy's and Robert F. Kennedy's assassinations held by the library. Although the library does not have a complete collection, it has a strong representative collection.[51]

Use

The library is open to scholars and interested members of the general public. The number of museum visitors in 1985 was 252,617; the number of research visits was 2,110.

Staff

The staff consists of eighteen professional staff members (seven archivists, one librarian and ten others) and thirty-seven nonprofessionals (seven technical assistants, five clerks, and twenty-five others).

Budget

The appropriated operating funds for a three-year period were: $885,000 for fiscal year 1983, $843,000 for fiscal year 1984, and $870,000 for fiscal year 1985.

LYNDON B. JOHNSON PRESIDENTIAL LIBRARY

The Lyndon Baines Johnson Library was dedicated and opened to the public on May 22, 1971. It is located on the high eastern portion of the University of Texas campus, Austin, Texas, on a 30-acre site. Ground was broken for the library in September 1967. The library adjoins Sid Richardson Hall, which houses the Lyndon Baines Johnson School of Public Affairs. This closeness facilitates an interaction between these two establishments, the library providing important resources for study and research undertaken at the school.

Several other places had offered facilities to house the library. The president's alma mater, Southwest Texas State University in San Marcos, was considered as a site, as was Johnson City, President Johnson's boyhood town. But Austin was selected because the president became convinced that his library could best develop and be of advantage to the largest number of people if it was located in an easily accessible city with a multifaceted campus.

The building,[52] a melding of museum and library, is 100,000 square feet in size.[53] It consists of eight stories and a basement. Lady Bird Johnson, the president's wife, who had a big part in all stages of the development of the library, did not want the Johnson papers to appear "grey, anonymous, box after box, identically bound, hidden from the world on shelves behind locked doors. . . ."[54] "The dramatic display of documents overlooking the Great Hall of the Lyndon Baines Johnson Library and Museum—four stories of red buckram boxes, each bearing a gold presidential seal—embodies a different spirit."[55]

In the collection, there are nearly 35 million pages of papers, of which about 30 million were produced during the presidency, about 2,455,800 before the presidency, and about 1,707,750 after the presidency. The collection includes about 600,000 papers from the family. Also included are papers from the presidential advisers and members of the cabinet and other persons associated with President Johnson.

In his deed of gift, Lyndon B. Johnson stipulated that all papers except those classified for security reasons should be made available for study unless they contained material that might embarrass or harass living persons. Less than 1 percent of the papers received by 1977 were closed.[56] Those closed are periodically reviewed and opened when the reason for closing them has been removed—usually the case when a person to whom reference has been made has died.

The Lyndon Baines Johnson Library intends to continue acquiring materials. Since they have to be examined for possible closure, the reviewing process has to remain open-ended. In accordance with a priority system for reviewing, the presidential papers are examined first, then Johnson's congressional papers, and then those from his vice-presidency. Last reviewed are the papers from donors.

Over a million of the papers in the library are concerned with foreign affairs and are classified confidential. They must be declassified before they can be made available to users.[57]

The collection includes manuscripts and archival materials, books and periodicals, audiovisual records, and oral history interviews.[58] Most of the materials were originated or received by the president, but a considerable number of papers were donated by associates, friends, and others who could make a contribution to the understanding of Johnson's complex personality or to the Johnson era in general.

Professional or honorary titles of individuals who contributed papers are those they had during the periods covered by the papers. A number of individuals who were staff members are represented by both papers and files. Papers are the materials donated directly to the library by individuals or their heirs. Files are materials left in the White House; they have come to the library as part of the Johnson papers.

The major periods to which the materials are assigned are prepresidential, presidential, and postpresidential.

The prepresidential papers can be subdivided as follows:

House of Representatives papers, 1937–1949.

Senate papers, 1949–1961.

Vice-presidential papers, 1961–1963.

Each of these units is subdivided into categories that reflect Johnson's interests and involvements during the period covered. For example, the House of Representatives papers have a file on political correspondence covering campaigns from 1937 to 1948. They also contain a file on general correspondence, which includes commendations to and from Johnson, complimentary references, and gifts and donations. A case file deals with, among other matters, military branches, federal agencies, veterans, and constituents.

For the presidential papers, 1963–1969 the White House Central Files are the largest and most comprehensive files. They hold most nonclassified correspondence and memoranda. The subject file was maintained in two categories: executive and general. Executive material covers the items that are of particular importance because of their source or nature. General materials are those received from the public and handled at a lower level of government. Unlike several other presidents, Lyndon Baines Johnson did not maintain a separate office file. Thus the name file is most important because it serves as an index to the subject file. The names of the several other files reveal their respective scope and functions: National Security Files, President's Staff Files, and White House Social Files.

The postpresidential files, 1969–1973 are assigned to a Subject File, Name File, Chronological File, and Storage File (the file designations that had been used for the papers created during the presidency). For this period, there are also Correspondence and Files sections, the Willie Day Taylor Files, and the Files from the ranch office at the time of the president's death.

The importance of a presidential library for the understanding of political and other social conditions of the president's home state is evidenced by a study by Claudia Wilson Anderson, which refers to the several files that throw light on Johnson's long and varied career.[59] She refers in particular to papers that give a full and sometimes intimate picture of Texas politics, such as the Byrne Skelton papers, which reveal the labor-liberal and conservative rivalries in the Texas Democratic party in 1956. Then she emphasizes how important the Name Files and the Subject Files prove in uncovering leading Texans and their specific roles and areas of involvement in Texas life. Anderson also points out that the large collection of about 1,500 interviews can be analyzed for their relevance to Texas. They give a good pictue of life in central Texas, revealing politics in depth, the problems of growing up in Texas, and the significance of tradition.

Microfilming of Papers

Microfilming has been undertaken by University Publications of America. Categories already microfilmed or considered for filming are administrative histories (some have already been microfilmed); newspaper clippings; Lyndon Baines Johnson's daily diary (already microfilmed); and federal records (some already microfilmed).

Acquisition Policy

The objective is to increase the research potential of the library through the acquisition of historical material related to the president, his work, his family, and his associates. Materials appropriate for acquisition consist of textual, audiovisual, machine-readable, and three-dimensional items with a subject matter or physical relation to the president and his family.

Book Collection

This collection consists of nearly 15,000 items containing mainly titles dealing with Lyndon B. Johnson's career, his family and his presidency, the U.S. presidency in general, and twentieth-century U.S. history. The library also has about 3,700 journal issues and current subscriptions to over eighteen journals, mainly historical.

Books are classified in accordance with the Library of Congress scheme. Current periodicals are filed alphabetically by title in the research room. Periodical articles are filed alphabetically by author in the Vertical File.

Audiovisual Collection

The audiovisual component of the collection includes over 599,000 still photographs, over 824,700 feet of film, as well as videotapes and audiotapes as noted in table 2.

The motion pictures have come from many sources. The largest number have been produced by government departments. Some have been produced by or commissioned for the library. Special items include an orientation film about the library prepared by the staff and a biography of former President Johnson. Included are films from various other sources, among them foreign governments.

Sound recording tapes include addresses, speeches, and remarks by Lyndon B. Johnson from the prepresidential to the postpresidential period, congressional briefings, addresses and remarks by President John F. Kennedy, and remarks by secretaries of several government departments. There are also some tapes received from the Democratic National Committee and the 1964 Democratic and the 1964 Republican national conventions.

The videotape collection includes videotapes of Walter Rostow's lectures and the Lyndon Baines Johnson Library series, an expanding series of coverage of special events sponsored by the library.

Oral History

From 1968 to 1984, 1,479 interviews comprising 46,791 pages were conducted with 995 individuals. One hundred twenty-nine of the interviews involving 91 individuals were conducted during 1983–1984. As of November 1984, 962 were available for use. Fifty-six have been deeded to the library but are restricted and thus not yet available to researchers. The remaining 461 are still in the processing stage.

It is probable that the interview program will continue until about 1989 at the present pace. By that time, it is assumed that the review program will be practically completed, and only a few interviews are likely to be conducted in subsequent years.[60]

Museum Services

The Lyndon B. Johnson Library holds nearly 38,000 museum objects, classified by item, donor, and date. A number of the objects are displayed in exhibits; some are permanent, and others are special and traveling exhibits.

Most of the exhibits illustrate significant events in Johnson's life, although some focus on other aspects of the American political and social scene. The titles of a few of the museum exhibits illustrate the range they cover: "A Family Album" shows Lady Bird, LBJ, and their daughters with their families. "Treasures from around the World" brings a selection of gifts given to the president by leaders of other nations. The exhibit "American Handiwork" contains gifts from people across the nation to the president. "The Great Society" exhibit depicts the major social programs of the Johnson administration. "Exhibits on Foreign Affairs" attempts to give a picture of foreign policy as a whole, focusing on the Vietnam War. Among exhibits dealing with other aspects of American life are "Honoring the Sesquicentennial of Texas," "The Statue of Liberty," and "Theodore," devoted to the life and career of President Theodore Roosevelt.[61]

Staff

The total number of staff is twenty-nine, three of whom are part-time. The professional employees consist of nine archivists (two of the nine archivists have M.L.S. degrees but do not serve as librarians), and such other staff members as audiovisual archivists, oral historian, technical services chief, museum curator, exhibit specialist, and museum registrar. The nonprofessional staff consists of one library aide, one clerk, and two secretaries. To supplement the federally paid staff, the Lyndon Baines Johnson Foundation pays the salaries of about ten persons who work on library programs.

Use of Library

During 1985, there were 2,301 researcher visits. The number of new researchers was 322. Six hundred eighty-one received copies of documents by mail. During the same period the number of museum visitors was 402,768. The Johnson Library does not charge any admission fee.

Budget

The annual appropriations since 1983 are $860,000 for fiscal year 1983, $891,000 for fiscal year 1984, and $920,000 for 1985.

Publications

Among the publications issued by the LBJ Library, one deserves to be singled out as a bibliographical source for many aspects of Lyndon B. Johnson's life and times: *Lyndon B. Johnson: A Bibliography*, compiled by the staff of the LBJ Library (1984).

A number of activities not funded by the federal government have been supported by the Lyndon Baines Johnson Foundation through the Friends of the Lyndon B. Johnson Library. Examples are the production of "The Journey of Lyndon Johnson," a documentary film on Johnson's life and career, completed in 1974, and a film entitled, "The First Lady: A Portrait of Lady Bird Johnson," released in 1981. The Friends of the Library have sponsored symposia that dealt with such topics as "Equal Opportunity in the United States" and "The International Challenge of the 1980's." These programs have generally attracted outstanding panel members. The Distinguished Lectures series, established through a grant from the Moody Foundation, has brought prominent figures to the library. The series was inaugurated with an address by Harold Wilson, former British prime minister, followed by such distinguished lecturers as Averell Harriman, Elliott Richardson, Henry Kissinger, and Dean Rusk. Admission to these events, which usually draw large crowds, is free. The Oral History Project is another important program sponsored by the Friends of the Library.

Also noteworthy is the national tribute to Lady Bird Johnson, held in the library on December 11, 1977, which culminated in a drive to establish a permanent endowment.

Volunteer Program

The Lyndon B. Johnson Library and Museum has ninety-nine volunteers. Of these, seventy-one are docents, giving tours to visitors. The others help in other areas of the library, taking slide shows on museum exhibits to nursing homes and senior citizen groups, and preparing educational materials.[62]

Grants-in-Aid

By virtue of a grant from the Moody Foundation of Galveston, Texas, the Lyndon Baines Johnson Foundation has been able to make available annually since 1974 grants for research involving use of the library's resources.[63] There were twenty-six recipients for the year 1984–1985. A total of $17,920 was distributed among them to assist in defraying travel and living expenses.

NIXON PRESIDENTIAL MATERIALS PROJECT

The treatment of the Nixon presidential materials is governed by Title I of the Presidential Recordings and Materials Preservation Act.[64] This law stipulates that the custody of the Nixon materials "shall be maintained in Washington, District of Columbia, or its metropolitan area."[65] The location chosen meets this requirement. The project is housed in a brick and concrete warehouse, built in the 1970s and located in Alexandria, Virginia.[66] The Nixon project occupies about 35,000 square feet of floor space in an office building that contains about 88,000 square feet of office space.[67] Ultimately a permanent library structure will be erected in San Clemente, California. In the meantime, the spacious warehouse will accommodate materials, staff, and users.

Nixon materials cover all kinds of data relating to President Richard M. Nixon. Some are subject to government custody. Figure 1 (in Chapter 1) lists the kinds of materials and their intended disposition.

All materials held at the Alexandria depository were produced or received during Nixon's presidency. All prepresidential materials are stored in the Federal Archives and Records Center at Laguna Miguel, California. The Nixon project has no personal (private) papers from family members, only those of an official nature. In accordance with the provisions of the act and its implementing regulations, the staff worked first on materials identified with Watergate. Since these items have to be examined closely, the progress has been slow. The archivists processing materials of presidents prior to Nixon followed a different sequence. First they reviewed noncontroversial materials, which could be handled relatively quickly; then they turned to the more volatile subjects contained in papers of the president and inner White House figures.

Like the materials of his predecessors, the Nixon materials were placed in typical files, which have been fully described by Ronald J. Plavchan.[68] Usually the quantities contained in each file and subfile have been given.

The largest files are the White House Central Files. This unit maintains a central filing and retrieval system for the president and his staff. It consists of many kinds of materials—correspondence, memoranda, reports, telegrams, courtesy messages, invitations—in short, materials generated or received by the White House.

Periodically the files of the White House staff members and their offices were forwarded to the White House Central Files for storage and integration. These staff members files include memoranda, correspondence, telegrams, and briefing papers. The subject content varies and reflects the responsibilities and concerns of the officials. A number of files or portions of files that were part of the White House Central Files were separated out and administered by the Special Files Unit created in 1972 to provide storage for materials considered sensitive. The Special Files Unit contains all records of the president's secretary, Rose Mary Woods, the entire daily diary of the president, and the files from the offices of H. R. Haldeman, John Ehrlichman, John Dean, and Charles Colson. In addition, portions of files of over fifty staff members were transferred to the Special Files unit.

Another file consists of donated materials. As of March 1984, it comprised 137 collections solicited and received during the Nixon administration by the office of Presidential Papers and Archives, a liaison office of the National Archives within the White House. It is expected that this collection will increase considerably when the Nixon project institutes a solicitation program. Most of the donated materials so far obtained are from high officials of the first Nixon administration.

Records from various federal agencies and organizations in the executive department have been accessioned by the National Archives. The National Archives have transferred some of these records to the Nixon project because of the likelihood that they may be useful to researchers in conjunction with their use of presidential materials. Considered for transfer are, for example, records of task forces, boards, and committees that reported directly to the president, as well as records from other government departments whose materials are closely related to Nixon materials.

The Federal Records Files also contain the materials from the Watergate special prosecutor's project. They consist of the files of the archival search team that handled requests for information from the special prosecution force.

The Oral History project was conducted by members of the National Archives. They administered exit interviews to 249 departing members of the White House staff.

Gifts

Of great importance for the museum activities of the projected Nixon presidential library are gifts, both domestic and foreign. Most of the domestic gifts (about 20,000) are Mr. Nixon's personal property, and it will be up to him whether to donate them to the government. However, in accordance with the Foreign Gifts and Donations Act of 1966, foreign gifts exceeding $50 in value are government property. The foreign gifts number 951 items, all in government custody. The gifts were arranged by the White House gift unit, usually on a chronological basis by date of receipt.

Audiovisual Collection

The still photographs file contains approximately 435,000 photographs taken by the official White House photographers. They document both official and social activities. In addition there is a prepresidential photo file of about 1,200 items covering the years 1950–1968.

Created by the White House Communications Agency (WHCA), sound recordings form the largest group in this category and cover addresses and remarks by Vice-Presidents Spiro Agnew and Gerald Ford, selected speeches by the First Lady and other family members, the China advance trip telecommunications, and the complete recorded broadcasts of the Watergate hearings of the Select Committee on Presidential Campaign Activities.

A film unit consisting of films produced by the Naval Photographic Center covers selected activities of President Nixon, including diplomatic and social events. Another film unit is composed of 16 mm films presented to the White House by various sources.

The WHCA video collection consists of 4,807 broadcast-quality quadriplex videotapes comprising 3,900 hours of playing time. They are recordings of commercial stations and the Public Broadcasting

Service (PBS). They include all televised public affairs programs, actualities, and weekly summaries of each major television network's morning and evening news programs. In addition, there is a smaller file group consisting of video recordings in various formats and from various sources.

The presidential election campaign audiovisual collection deserves special consideration. It includes sound recordings, video recordings, and motion film produced by the Nixon Agnew Committee and the Committee to Elect the President.

White House Tapes

In February 1971, the Technical Services Division of the Secret Service began installing a sound-activated taping system in the White House complex. Other recording stations were added, and eventually there were seven in operation in these locations: the Oval Office, the president's office in the Old Executive Office Building, the cabinet room, three White House telephones, and Camp David. The system was removed in July 1973.

There are 950 original reels, 415 White House duplicates, and 4,000 reels of enhanced master tape. In 1977 the National Archives took custody of the White House tapes. Since assuming custody, the Nixon project has duplicated the whole series, sound-enhanced each tape, and prepared a draft topic outline for each tape. The whole group of White House tapes engendered approximately 25,000 pages of topic outlines. Staff members of the Nixon project review the tapes for public access and for possible restrictions.

A group of 718 dictabelts consists of dictated memos, letters and speeches, recorded meetings, and telephone conversations, mainly recorded by the president. Some were recorded by H. R. Haldeman, John D. Ehrlichman, and several other high officials.

The original set has been duplicated by 718 reel-to-reel duplicates and 718 cassette duplicates.

Book Collection

The Nixon project reference books collection is estimated at 9,000 volumes. Most titles deal with the Nixon administration and with modern history. They were collected by representatives of the National Archives for staff and researcher use.

The president's gift book collection, estimated at 10,000 volumes, consists largely of books donated to Nixon during his presidency by authors, as well as other persons.

Government Printing Office Publications

It has been the practice of the Government Printing Office (GPO) to send at least one copy of every publication it prints during a particular presidency for eventual deposit to the National Archives for storage and eventual deposit in a presidential library. It is es- timated that GPO publications covering 3,000 square feet have been delivered to the Nixon project.[69] "Because GPO publications vary so greatly in size from bound volumes to pamphlets, as well as the fact that sometimes Presidential Projects receive multiple copies, the only way to determine the total volumes would be to open each Federal Record Center carton and count the items. For the time being we prefer to use the estimated amount."[70]

Microfilming of Papers

There are no firm plans to microfilm the presidential papers; how- ever, there has been some discussion about microfilming materials regarded as heavily used by researchers or with a high degree of intrinsic value, such as the President's Handwriting File.

Use

The materials are not freely accessible as are the materials in already existing presidential libraries. Access to the Nixon presi- dential materials is governed by the Presidential Recordings and Material Preservation Act and the implementing regulations (spe- cial access regulations). Until recently only a small quantity of pa- pers was accessible to the general public. More extensive use should become possible now that pertinent federal regulations have been published.[71]

Staff

As of early 1985, the staff consisted of sixteen archivists and five archives technicians. Two of the archivists have library experience, but they perform largely archival functions.

Budget

The budget figures for a three-year period are $628,000 for fiscal year 1983, $613,000 for fiscal year 1984, and $706,000 for fiscal year 1985.

GERALD R. FORD PRESIDENTIAL LIBRARY AND THE GERALD R. FORD MUSEUM

The Gerald R. Ford Presidential Library setup differs from that of all other presidential libraries. The Ford Library's two components are in different cities. The archives component is located in the university setting of Ann Arbor, Michigan, and the museum component is in Grand Rapids, Michigan, Ford's hometown and district he represented while in Congress.

The Gerald R. Ford library building project began in 1977, and the library was dedicated on April 27, 1981.[72] It is a low-lying two-story brick and bronze glass structure on the University of Michigan's North Campus, south of the Bentley Historical Library. The firm that designed the Bentley Library also designed the Ford Library. Nearly all phases of construction of the Ford Library, its scale, and its design philosophy complement the Bentley Library.

The Ford Library is about 40,000 square feet in size, and its construction cost was $4,289,669. The library is operated by the National Archives and Records Service, but the building remains the property of the University of Michigan.

By the opening, some 14,000 persons had contributed to the private fund-raising campaign, which had netted about $11,950,000. The funds were used for the construction of the library and the museum.

President Ford donated by a deed of gift to the United States government his congressional, vice-presidential, and presidential papers on December 13, 1976.[73] Since completing his term of office, Gerald R. Ford has augmented the collections by donating various personal and postpresidential materials.

The Congressional Files cover the period 1948–1973. In 1948 Ford was first elected from Michigan's Fifth Congressional District. He was House minority leader from 1965 to 1973. Until 1964, the Ford congressional office destroyed many of the noncurrent files. In 1964, the Michigan Historical Collections Office asked Ford to deposit his papers there. These papers remained with the Michigan Historical Collections only for a limited time; they were transferred to the Gerald R. Ford Presidential Library after its establishment.

The Vice-Presidential Files date from Ford's nomination to the office by President Nixon in October 1973 to replace Vice-President Agnew, and they conclude with his being appointed president in 1974. The papers include little material on Ford's transition to his Presidency. The papers crated and received during the presidency (1974–1977) represent the core of the collection. About 14 million pages were produced during the presidency, about 2.5 million pages before the presidency, and about 400,000 pages after the presidency. The presidential family has contributed about 150,000 pages, almost exclusively from Ford's wife, Betty Ford.

The White House staff provided 400,000 pages by donations separate from President Ford's. About a million pages of papers were supplied by associates and former government officials. The library holds about 25,000 pages of selected federal agency records.

With regard to the papers that originated during the presidency, the file system created by the White House was retained. In some instances, the White House found it desirable to reconstruct and perfect an arrangement.

The White House Central Files (WHCF) was the common file system shared by the president and his staff. Along with the bulk of generally accessible materials, this file contains a number of defense and foreign policy materials. These materials were largely unclassified or were classified confidential.

The Subject File of the WHCF is an important search device; however, the index is idiosyncratic and must be used with caution.

The Name File of the WHCF is primarily a name index to the Subject File. It indexes prominent as well as nonprominent citizens, members of Congress, and government officials. The WHCF Chronological File contains chronologically arranged copies of selected outgoing documents.

The Bulk Mail File of the WHCF consists largely of routine letters, telegrams, post cards, greeting cards, and so forth. These letters were either not answered or answered by form letter only. The library has retained only representative samples of these items.

The Social Office Files of the WHCF represent a separate entity consisting of Subject File, Name File, Chronological File, and Bulk Mail File maintained in support of the Social Office in the White House East Wing. It served the First Lady, her staff, and the Ford children.

In addition to using and depositing materials in the WHCF, most White House staff members kept files in their own offices. These files are grouped by offices and thereunder by the unit or individual who created the files. Within this category are, among others, the files of the offices of the counsel of the president and of the counsellors to the President, domestic affairs assistant, economic affairs assistant, the national security adviser, and the presidential personnel office.

The Post-Presidential Office Files unit containing materials from 1977 to the present is expanding because the library continues to receive materials from Ford that relate to his postpresidential activities. This unit also has personal papers from 1913 to the present, excluding materials from the Ford White House.

The library has about thirty collections of donated papers and records that relate to Ford's private and public life and generally to issues regarding his presidency.

The library continues to seek materials that document Ford's life, his presidency, and public issues contemporaneous with his presidency.

Audiovisual Materials

The library has still pictures, films, and videotapes and audiotapes in the quantities listed in table 2. These items are from many sources: from Gerald Ford's associates in government and politics, from private individuals, and from government agencies.

The audiovisual materials mirror many aspects of Ford's private and public life, but most of the collections focus on Ford's years in the presidency.

Ford's day-to-day activities were recorded by the White House Photographic Office. David Kennerly and four other photographers alone produced about 283,000 negatives. Users may obtain contact sheets of these negatives for reference.

Other noteworthy still photograph collections are the Gerald R. Ford Scrapbook Photographs and the Gerald R. Ford Congressional Photograph Collection. The Scrapbook Collection consists of over 4,000 photographs that cover the years 1913–1984. The Ford Congressional Photograph Collection, consisting of 4,800 photographs, documents Ford's twenty-five years in Congress and for this period parallels the Scrapbook Collection.

Motion picture film was largely produced by the Naval Photographic Center and by navy film crews. All film is 16 mm color. Some of the film has soundtrack. Audiotape and videotape were nearly exclusively created by the White House Communications Agency. The tapes contain the public statements and television appearances recorded during Ford's presidency. The 2,600 audiotapes include speeches, impromptu remarks, and press briefings, as well as family tapes. The 765 videotapes are records of presidential speeches, press conferences, and daily news reports from the three major networks.

Oral Histories

So far this collection is very small. It consists of interviews of eight persons, seven of whom were Grand Rapids associates of the president. They discussed President Ford's involvement in the political and social life of Grand Rapids.

Book Collection

This collection of about 8,600 volumes is arranged by Library of Congress classification and includes all kinds of accounts, scholarly and popular, that concern Ford's presidency and the rest of his career. The collection also contains basic reference works and works on the modern presidency.

Among the printed sources are federal government publications such as congressional hearings, reports, and selected special publications.

The Serials Collection has hard or microfilm copies of the *New York Times* and other newspapers for the period 1973–1974. The file of the *Grand Rapids Press* runs from 1948 to 1960. The library also subscribes to a small number of archival and political science newsletters and journals. They are in the process of being cataloged by the Library of Congress scheme.

The Vertical File contains a subject file of news clippings, articles, pamphlets, and photocopies of various general interest items.

The Staff

The Ann Arbor library staff is composed of ten full-time equivalent archivists and 1.75 full-time equivalent nonprofessional staff members.

Use

In 1985 the library and museum had 114,214 museum visitors and 977 researcher visits. During its first full year of operation, the museum attracted about 400,000 visitors. To facilitate use of recently opened materials, the library has published *Newsletter to Researchers*, which highlights selected recent and planned openings of historical materials.[74]

Budget

The appropriated funds for a three-year period were $572,000 for fiscal year 1983, $611,00 for fiscal year 1984, and $633,00 for fiscal year 1985. These amounts do not include trust fund money. Such money comes from admissions fees, sales desk revenues, and charges for reproducing materials for individual researchers.

Of the total amount available, 77 percent goes for personnel. The balance is generally earmarked at the director's discretion.

Figures do not include expenditures by the Gerald R. Ford Foundation in support of conferences, symposia, and research.

Conferences, Tours, and Other Services

The library offers presentations and tours to interested groups. It conducts class sessions in archival research and archival administration to students from junior high to the graduate school level.

In conjunction with the Gerald R. Ford Foundation, the library sponsors conferences, symposia, and research. A notable symposium held in Grand Rapids in April 1984 was "Modern First Ladies: Private Lives and Public Duties." Among those participating were Robert M. Warner, archivist of the United States, and James E. O'Neill, assistant archivist for presidential libraries.[75]

In addition to supporting conferences and symposia, the Gerald R. Ford Foundation sponsors exhibits and supports special projects to augment the holdings of the library and the museum. Further, the foundation offers grants up to $2,000 for research based primarily on the collection in the Gerald R. Ford Library.[76]

Gerald R. Ford Museum

The Ford Museum, the sister institution of the library, is located in Grand Rapids on the west bank of the Grand River.[77] It is a two-story building of sandblasted concrete in triangular shape with a 300-feet east wall of glass.

The museum covers 40,00 square feet and cost $7.2 million. It was opened to the public in September 1981. Most of the museum objects are related to the life and career of Ford.[78] The objects are arranged under a date and object number system developed by the museum staff.

Visitors usually begin their tour at the first floor theater by viewing the movie, *Gerald R. Ford: The Presidency Restored.*

The museum has permanent and changing exhibits. The permanent exhibits trace Ford's life from his boyhood to the 1976 election campaign. These exhibits consist of three sections: boyhood, Congress, and the presidency. The presidency section is allotted about half of the permanent exhibit space. The congressional section of the permanent exhibits includes a wall diagram that illustrates the path a bill takes from introduction through House and Senate. Also included in the diagram are a House and a Senate resolution, cartoon portrayals of subcommittee hearings, floor debates, House-Senate conference committee proceedings, measures leading to a public law, and options a president has when legislation reaches his office.

Another permanent exhibit is a full-scale exact reproduction of the Oval Office.

The changing exhibits generally expand on the topics introduced in the permanent exhibits or deal with topics related to recent U.S. history. An example is "Quilts: A Bicentennial Collection." This exhibit consisted of fifteen quilts from the museum's collection and photographs, letters, and newspaper clippings associated with the quilts when presented to President and/or Mrs. Ford. Another important exhibit was "Photographing the President." The preparation of this exhibit was a cooperative enterprise involving not only the staffs of the Ford Library and the Ford Museum but also individuals from other presidential libraries and the two presidential materials projects. Over fifty photographs were selected to show presidents in their many roles.[79]

A noteworthy changing exhibit was "Diplomatic Bicentennial"; It celebrated the two hundredth anniversary of the signing of the Treaty of Amity and Commerce between the United States and the Netherlands.

The museum offers a variety of tours and public programs, differentiated by such criteria as age and education levels. Currently the museum makes available three tours: "General Tour," "Presidential Elections," and "How Our Laws Are Made."

Public programs include conferences, such as "Press and the Presidency." There are evening lectures, public forums, and the National Issues Forum cosponsored with the Kettering Foundation and the Great Decisions lecture series, cosponsored with the World Affairs Council of West Michigan.

The museum staff consists of eleven persons: a curator, a registrar, a designer, a director of the education program, a woodcrafter, an administrative assistant, a sales desk manager, and four sales desk clerks.

During the first year, nearly 400,000 persons visited the museum. After the first year, the number of visitors was about 130,000 per year.

JIMMY CARTER PRESIDENTIAL LIBRARY

In its temporary stages the Jimmy Carter Presidential Library was called the Carter Presidential Materials Project.

On January 20 and 21, 1981, the materials that form the core of the Carter collection were transferred from the White House to a temporary location in Atlanta, Georgia.[80] On January 31, 1981, President Carter deeded the materials to the United States. They were accepted by the U.S. archivist in February 1981. A corporation to raise funds for establishing a library building was formed in June 1981, and a building design was selected in December 1981. Ground for the building located in Atlanta was broken on October 2, 1984. The building was dedicated on October 1, 1986. The museum section was opened to the public the following day. The Library was scheduled to open for research six to eight weeks after that.

The anticipated cost of the building is $25 million. The building plan provides for a structure that will be 70,000 square feet in size. The building will have two main floors that adjoin four short floors of stacks.

The museum exhibit area is segregated from the rest of the building and has a separate entrance.

From the exterior, the building appears to be round, but stack and work areas below ground level (about one-half of the building) are square.

The bulk of the collection of papers consists of about 27 million pages produced during Carter's presidency, about 5,000 pages produced before the presidency, and about 500,000 produced after the presidency. The last group is still growing. The collection contains about 5,000 pages of materials from the president's family, mainly from Carter's wife, Rosalynn Carter. Presidential advisers too have contributed to the collection.

The book collection is still quite small but growing.

The audiovisual holdings are composed of still pictures, motion pictures, and videotapes and audiotapes, as noted on table 2. The photographs number about 1.5 million—600,000 in black and white and 900,000 in color.

The terms of President Carter's letter of gift provide that the materials are closed to research while the initial processing is done. Exceptions are being made only with Carter's permission. From 1981 to the end of 1984, only three or four researchers had been granted such permission. Once all initial processing is completed, the materials will be freely available to any researcher. Processing priorities will determine the sequence in which the papers become available to the user.

Acquisition Policy

The acquisition policy, and the solicitation efforts based on this policy, fall into four categories. They concern, in order of precedence:

1. Materials of Jimmy Carter and Rosalynn Carter.

2. Materials of major figures and political and social associates and acquaintances.

3. Materials of similar figures of secondary importance.

4. Materials of President Carter's family.

Every reasonable effort will be made with regard to materials in categories 1 and 2. For the time being, the efforts with regard to President and Mrs. Carter's papers may be described as passive efforts, which are to ensure that nothing is destoryed or otherwise disposed without the Carter project's having had an opportunity to evaluate the materials. It is expected that the president will become involved in obtaining materials in category 2.

Category 3 materials will be sought continuously but not aggressively. For Category 4 solicitation will proceed selectively. Only contributions that can enhance the documentation of Mr. and Mrs. Carter's careers and their family histories will be sought.

The acquisition of books and other secondary sources will be affected by the location of the Carter Library. Atlanta is a city rich in library resources. Therefore the project will attempt to be a primary resource only for material dealing directly with Carter and his administration but in general not for Carter-related materials because these materials are expected to be found in other Atlanta libraries. However, pamphlets and other fugitive materials relating to Mr. and Mrs. Carter would be collected if other libraries are not likely to have such items.

The library will acquire reference books and other items that it needs for day-to-day operations.

Museum

Museum objects, numbering about 40,000 items, will be housed in a separate part of the building.

Staff

The professional staff numbers eight (seven and one-half archivists and one-half librarian). The nonprofessional staff has two members.

Budget

The figures for appropriated funds for the 1983–1985 period are $305,000 for 1983, $328,000 for 1984, and $405,000 for 1985. About 90 percent of the budget is for staff costs.

Notes

1. There are many accounts describing the reasons for establishment of the FDR library, its role, its functions and its scope. See, for instance, H. G. Jones, *The Records of a Nation: Their Management, Preservation and Use* (New York: Atheneum, 1969), pp. 144–55; Herman Kahn, "The Presidential Library—A New Institution," *Special Libraries* 50, no. 3 (March 1959): 106–13; R. D. W. Connor, "The Franklin D. Roosevelt Library," *American Archivist* 3, no. 2 (April 1940): 81–92; Waldo G. Leland, "The Creation of the Franklin D. Roosevelt Library: A Personal Narrative," *American Archivist* 18, no. 1 (January 1955): 11–31; Donald R. McCoy, "The Beginnings of the Franklin D. Roosevelt Library," *Prologue* 7 (Fall 1975): 137–50.

2. Jones, *Records of a Nation*, p. 146.

3. Ibid., pp. 150–51.

4. S.J. Res. 118, H.J. Res. 268, approved as Public Res. 30, 76th Cong., July 18, 1939.

5. Franklin D. Roosevelt Library, *Historical Materials in the Franklin D. Roosevelt Library* (Hyde Park, N.Y.: Franklin D. Roosevelt Library, 1982).

6. *The Franklin D. Roosevelt Library and Museum* (Hyde Park, N.Y.: Franklin D. Roosevelt Library, n.d.).

7. Office of Chief of Files (unnumbered page from a report by Fred W. Shipman).

8. Information based on "Acquisition and Solicitation Policy for the Franklin D. Roosevelt Library."

9. Ibid., p. 2.

10. Roosevelt Library, *Historical Materials*, pp. 20–23.

11. Franklin D. Roosevelt Library. [Audio Visual Materials]: Motion Pictures, 1912–1980; Sound Recordings, 1913–1980; Still Pictures 1870-Present.

12. *The Franklin D. Roosevelt Library and Museum* (folder).

13. Public Law 373, 84th Cong., 69 Stat. 965–966 44 USC 2107 et. seq.

14. Pub. Res. 30, 76th Cong., 53 Stat. 1062.

15. "The Harry S. Truman Library" [description of building, holdings, use], p. 2.

16. For a detailed description of the materials included in the various files, see Harry S. Truman Library, *Historical Materials in the Harry S. Truman Library* (Independence, Mo.: Harry S. Truman Library, 1982), pp. 5–6.

17. Ibid., p. 3.

18. Ibid., pp. 2, 39–42.

19. Ibid., p. 42.

20. Ibid., pp. 2, 43–65.

21. Harry S. Truman Library, *Museum Tour Plan* (Independence, Mo.: Harry S. Truman Library, n.d.)., folder; "The Harry S. Truman Library and Museum" (Independence, Mo.: Harry S. Truman Library and Museum n.d.), folder.

22. Truman Library, *Historical Materials*, p. 10.

23. U.S. Department of the Interior, National Park Service, "Herbert Hoover: National Historic Site, Iowa" (Washington, 1982), folder; William T. Anderson, "Hoover Historical Site: Hiding behind the Highway Signs," *Home and Away—Iowa* (July-August 1983): 16H-P; Hoover Presidential Library Association, *Herbert Hoover: The Uncommon Man* (n.p.: Hoover Presidential Library Association, 1974), p. 52; *The Herbert Hoover Presidential Library and Museum* (n.d.), folder.

24. Questionnaire reply, December 10, 1984.

25. Herbert Hoover Presidential Library, *Historical Materials in the Herbert Hoover Presidential Library*, (West Branch, Iowa: Herbert Hoover Presidential Library, 1983), p. v.

26. Ibid., pp. 5–6.

27. Ibid., p. 1.

28. *The Dwight D. Eisenhower Library* (Abilene, Kans.: National Archives and Records Service, n.d.), [p. 2.].

29. John E. Wickman, "The Dwight D. Eisenhower Library: Its Goal Is Infinity" *Special Libraries* (November 1969): 591.

30. Dwight D. Eisenhower Library, *Historical Materials in the Dwight D. Eisenhower Library* (Abilene, Kans.: Dwight D. Eisenhower Library, 1984), p. 76.

31. Ibid., p. 77.

32. Ibid., p. 2.

33. Ibid., p. 1.

34. Ibid., pp. 70–75.

35. Ibid., pp. 40–69.

36. Ibid., p. 5.

37. Robert G. Chenhall, *Nomenclature for Museum Cataloging* (Nashville: American Association for State and Local History, 1978).

38. Dan H. Fenn, Jr., "Launching the John F. Kennedy Library," *American Archivist* 42, no. 4 (October 1979): 429–42.

39. John F. Kennedy Library, *Historical Materials in the John Fitzgerald Kennedy Library* (Boston: Kennedy Library, 1981), p. 4.

40. Ibid., pp. 4–14.

41. Ibid., pp. 15–31.

42. Ibid., pp. 32–36.

43. Ibid., pp. 37–42; John F. Kennedy Library, "Audio Visual Collection" (Boston: John F. Kennedy Library [n.d.]).

44. Kennedy Library, *Historical Materials*, pp. 47–82; John F. Kennedy Library, "Oral History Program and the Use of Oral History Interviews" (Boston: John F. Kennedy Library, n.d.).

45. Kennnedy Library, *Historical Materials*, pp. 43–46.

46. Ibid., p. 44.

47. John F. Kennedy Library, "Collection Development Program" (Boston: John F. Kennedy Library, n.d.).

48. As, for instance, "Archival Accessions and Openings: October 1981 through June 1983."

49. Fenn, "Launching the John F. Kennedy Library," pp. 438, 441–42.

50. Ibid., pp. 441–42.

51. John F. Kennedy Library, "The Kennedy Assassinations: A Bibliography of Sources in the Kennedy Library" (Boston: John F. Kennedy Library, 1983).

52. For architectural details, see Lyndon Baines Johnson Library and Museum and Lyndon Baines Johnson School of Public Affairs, fact sheet (March 1985), p. 1; for cost and floor plans, see ibid., pp. 2–3.

53. Lyndon Baines Johnson Foundation, *The Lyndon Baines Johnson Library and Museum: A Progress Report* (Houston: Lyndon Baines Johnson Foundation 1982), p. 5.

54. Ibid., p. 2.

55. Ibid.

56. Harry Middleton, "The Lyndon Baines Johnson Presidential Library," *Texas Libraries* 39, no. 4 (Winter 1977): pp. 186–87.

57. Harry J. Middleton, "The LBJ Library," in *Discovery: Research and Scholarship at the University of Texas at Austin* (December 1979): 16.

58. The materials are listed, categorized, and described in Lyndon Baines Johnson Library, "Historical Materials in the Lyndon B. Johnson Library," draft list (June 1981).

59. Claudia W. Anderson, "The Lyndon Baines Johnson Library and Museum," in *Guide to the History of Texas.* (Westport, Conn: Greenwood Press, forthcoming).

60. "State of the LBJ Library, 1984," *Among Friends of LBJ, Newsletter of the Friends of the LBJ Library*, issue number 31, November 1, 1984, pp. 2–4.

61. *Welcome to the Lyndon Baines Johnson Library and Museum* (n.d.), folder; *Fact Sheet*, pp. 2–3; Johnson Foundation, *Progress Report*, "A Procession of History" and "A New Chapter"; *Among Friends of LBJ*, November 1, 1984, pp. 2–4.

62. *Among Friends of LBJ*, issue no. 31 (November 1, 1984) p. 3: *State of the Library*, (1984) p. 3.

63. "Research Grants Awarded to Twenty-six Scholars," *Among Friends of LBJ*, issue no. 31, November 1, 1984, p. 9; see also Lyndon Baines Johnson Foundation, "Grants in Aid of Research," *Information Sheet*.

64. Public Law 93–526, 44 USC 2107 note; 88 Stat. 1695, 14–19, 96, 97.

65. Public Law 93–526, sec. 101(a) (2).

66. Clement E. Vose, a member of the National Archives Advisory Council, has given an insightful account of a visit to the Nixon project. Among other matters, he describes the physical setup, pertinent legislation and court procedures,and the priority system for processing the materials and for releasing them to the public. Clement E. Vose, "The Nixon Project," *P.S.* (Summer 1983): 512–29.

67. Floor space figures were supplied by Ronald J. Plavchan, supervisory archivist, Nixon project. They differ from the figures given in Vose's article, cited in n. 66.

68. Ronald J. Plavchan, comp., "Holdings of the Nixon Presidential Materials Project" (March 1984). The material presented here draws heavily on Plavchan's work.

69. Ronald J. Plavchan, Letter to author, March 19, 1985.

70. Ibid.

71. *Federal Register*, February 28, 1986, 36 CFR, pt. 1275: "Preservation and Protection of and Access to the Presidential Historical Materials of the Nixon Administration."

72. University of Michigan, Ann Arbor, information service news release, April 27, 1981.

73. The files are described in Gerald R. Ford Library, *Historical Materials in the Gerald R. Ford Library*, comp. David Horrocks, William McNitt, and Richard Holzhausen (Ann Arbor, Mich.: Gerald R. Ford Library, 1984).

74. *Gerald R. Ford Library Newsletter to Researchers* (1983).

75. Gerald R. Ford Foundation, *Newsletter* (Summer 1984): [1–4].

76. Ibid., [p.5]; *Newsletter to Researchers*, (Fall 1984): 3–4.

77. *The Gerald R. Ford Museum* (Grand Rapids, Mich.: Gerald R. Ford Museum, n.d.).

78. The following information is based largely on William K. Jones, curator of Ford Museum, Letter to author, January 27, 1986.

79. *Photographing the Presidents: Herbert Hoover to Jimmy Carter* (Ann Arbor, Mich., and Grand Rapids, Mich.: Gerald R. Ford Library and Gerald R. Ford Museum, n.d.).

80. The following discussion is based on the questionnaire returns and on letters dated November 30, 1984, and December 18, 1985, and September 28, 1986, from Donald B. Schewe, director of the Carter Presidential Materials Project (now Jimmy Carter Presidential Library), to the author.

6

Papers of Presidents Preceding Hoover

Although there has been an intermittent interest in presidential papers throughout the history of the United States, in recent decades this interest has intensified. At various times, researchers have prepared holdings lists covering the early presidencies. Sometimes these lists included notes on provenance and other descriptive matter. Especially noteworthy is the pioneering effort of Rowland Buford.[1] Valuable listings and descriptions have also been prepared by Arnold D. Hirshon, among others.[2]

When Congress held hearings on the Presidential Libraries Act in 1955, it wished to be informed of the holdings and availability of the presidential papers from Washington's presidency to the time the hearings were held. A resume was prepared in the form of a table.[3]

After nearly twenty years, a new comprehensive table was prepared for hearings on the Public Documents Act.[4] This table, entitled "Depositories and Purchases of Presidential Papers," was compiled by Harold C. Relyea, specialist in American national government, Government division, Library of Congress, Congressional Research Service. This is the most up-to-date comprehensive tabulation that has come to my attention. Relyea informed me that he did not plan to update the table in the immediate future. He suggested that in most cases, major new additions will have occurred during the past decade only for the most recent presidents.[5] Similarly, Paul L. Broderick, assistant chief of the Manuscript Division, Library of Congress, observes that most of the presidential papers held by the Library of Congress "go back some time. The last major acquisitions of 20th century Presidents occurred really in the 1930's and 1940's."[6]

With certain modifications, this table has been reproduced here as table 5. The original table has entries for all presidents from Washington to Nixon; however, table 5 has dropped the entries for the collections beginning with Hoover since special presidential libraries have been built, or are scheduled to be built, for the collections of these recent presidents.

Table 5 shows for each president from Washington to Coolidge the papers still extant, the depositories, and in some instances the method of acquisition of a collection.

The table shows that the papers of the presidents can be found in many depositories. The Library of Congress is the most important depository for the papers of the presidents preceding Hoover. The Library of Congress has the bulk of the papers of twenty-three presidents, beginning with George Washington and ending with Calvin Coolidge.[7]

In 1903, the presidential papers that had been kept by the State Department were turned over to the Library of Congress, and presidential papers acquired subsequently were placed in the care of the Manuscript Division of the Library of Congress. The Manuscript Division began assuming an active role in obtaining presidential papers.[8] Table 6 shows the mode of acquisition and the date of acquisition of the papers by the Library of Congress.

It was generally felt that the presidential papers in the custody of the Library of Congress should be conveniently available to scholars and others. To this end, Congress authorized the Presidential Papers Program of the Library of Congress by public law 85–147, enacted August 16, 1957.[9] The next year, the Presidential Papers Section was established in the Manuscript Division. In accordance with the authorizing legislation, the section proceeded to arrange, index, and microfilm the presidential papers held by the Library of Congress, a job that took about fifteen years, from 1958 to 1973. It was begun with one of the smallest groups, the papers of Zachary Taylor. His papers were filmed and indexed in two years. Next fol-

Table 5
Depositories and Purchases of Presidential Papers

President	Depositories [1]	Purchases [2]	
George Washington (1732–99), President 1789–97.	The Library of Congress has some 800 volumes of letters, diaries, official papers, and other manuscripts. The Henry E. Huntington Library (San Marino, Calif.) has 450 letters. The Connecticut State Library has the extensive Trumbull correspondence. Other collections are in the Chicago Historical Society (150 pieces), the U.S. Naval Academy (15 pieces), Maryland Historical Society (62 pieces), Boston Public Library (5 vols.), Harvard College Library (88 pieces), William L. Clements Library (Ann Arbor) with 147 items, Detroit Public Library (part of the diary), Minnesota Historical Society (123 pieces), Princeton University Library, New Jersey State Library (3 items), Long Island Historical Society (123 pieces), Cornell University Library (80 pieces), Morristown National Historical Park (95 pieces), Columbia University Library (57 pieces, including parts of the diary), New York Historical Society (215 pieces), New York Public Libarry, Pierpont Morgan Library (New York, N.Y.) (114 items), Duke University Libraries (99 pieces), Historical Society of Pennsylvania, Virginia Historical Society (225 pieces), Virginia State Library, and William & Mary College (205 pieces). The Washington home, Mount Vernon, has family papers and diaries of the later years.	The Library of Congress acquired its papers in purchases totaling $45,000 in 1834 and 1849.	Y
John Adams (1735–1826), President 1797–1801.	The Adams papers are largely in the Massachusetts Historical Society, which has the diaries, the autobiography, and various manuscripts. There are 4 boxes of papers dated from 1776 to 1813. The Boston Public Library has some papers and some books with annotations by Adams. The post-presidential papers in the Harvard College Library are chiefly retrospective comments on the Revolution. There are scattered papers in the Columbia University Library, the Duke University Hospital Library, Princeton University Library, the Pierpont Morgan Library, and Historical Society of Pennsylvania.		X
Thomas Jefferson (1743–1826), President 1801–09.	The Library of Congress has 236 volumes of the correspondence, and the Massachusetts Historical Society has 77 volumes of papers and some of his record books. The University of Virginia has 2,500 items, Colonial Williamsburg 600 pieces, and William & Mary College 265 pieces. The Virginia Historical Society has 100 items, and there are some assorted papers in the Virginia State Library. Other collections are the Henry E. Huntington Library (800 pieces), the Historical Society of Delaware 14 items), the William L. Clements Library (91 pieces), the Missouri Historical Society (130 items), Princeton University Library, Columbia University Library (21 items), New York Historical Society (130 items), New York Public Library, Pierpont Morgan Library (245 pieces). Duke University Libraries (33 pieces), American Philosophic Society (Philadelphia), Historical Society of Pennsylvania, and the University of Texas (68 items).	Many of the 23,600 items held by the Library of Congress were purchased in 1848 for $20,000 from Thomas Jefferson Randolph, executor of the Jefferson estate. Fully half of the collection purchased at that time was returned, however, as being of too "personal" a nature for government acquisition. This returned cache of papers was ultimately dispersed by the heirs to friends, relatives, and collectors.	Y
James Madison (1751–1836), President 1809–17.	There are 114 boxes and 10 volumes of papers in the Library of Congress. The University of Virginia has 165 items, the New York Historical Society 134 pieces, and the Henry E. Huntington Library 104 pieces. There are smaller collections at the Virginia State Library, William & Mary College, the Virginia Historical Society, the Historical Society of Pennsylvania, the Pierpont Morgan Library, William L. Clements Library, and Princeton University Library. The New York Public Library has a collection of 390 items.	Of the approximately 10,000 items in the Madison collection held by the Library of Congress, most were acquired through 2 purchases from Mrs. Madison and one from the Chicago Historical Society. The cost of the 3 transactions amount to $65,000.	Y
James Monroe (1758–1831), President 1817–25.	Chief repositories are the Library of Congress with 40 volumes and 5 boxes, New York Public Library with 1,300 items, and the James Monroe Memorial Foundation (Fredericksburg, Va.) with an extensive and varied collection. There are also materials at William & Mary College (111 pieces), the University of Virginia (160 pieces), the New York Historical Society (50 items), the Pierpont Morgan Library (30 items), University of Pennsylvania Library (30 items), the Virginia Historical Society (35 items), and the Virginia State Library.	The Library of Congress holds 4,200 items which were acquired from the Monroe heirs in 1849 for $20,000.	

See footnotes at end of table.

Table 5 Continued

President	Depositories [1]	Purchases [2]	
John Quincy Adams (1767–1848), President 1825–29.	Most are in the Massachusetts Historical Society (some 15,000 diary pages and 6,300 letters). The Library of Congress has several boxes, and scattered items are in the New York Historical Society, the New York Public Library, and the Pierpont Morgan Library.		X
Andrew Jackson (1767–1845), President 1829–37.	The Library of Congress has a collection of over 340 volumes and boxes. The Tennessee State Library has 1,500 items, and the Tennessee Historical Society and the Jackson home, the Hermitage, have additional materials. Other collections are the Chicago Historical Society (450 items), New York Public Library (250 items), Pierpont Morgan Library (72 pieces), Duke University Libraries (50 items), Missouri Historical Society (40 items), Princeton University Library, and New York Historical Society.	Of the 20,000 items held by the Library of Congress, a small number of papers were Donated in 1903 by the F. P. Blair family; 2 purchases of papers were made an 1911 and 1932 for a total expenditure of $18,000. Some of Jackson's papers were lost in 1834 when the Hermitage burned.	Y
Martin Van Buren (1782–1862), President 1837–41.	The Library of Congress has 73 volumes and containers, and the New York State Library has a collection of letters. There are smaller collections in the Columbia County Historical Society (Kinderhook, N.Y.), the Pierpont Morgan Library and the Massachusetts Historical Society.	Van Buren's papers remained in the control of his family until 1904–05 when they were presented to the Library of Congress. The former President is thought to have destroyed many of his papers before his death.	
William Henry Harrison (1773–1841), President 1841.	Most are in the Library of Congress and Indiana State Library, but significant presidential writings are limited to his inaugural address.	A number of Harrison's records are thought to have been destroyed when his homestead burned in 1858.	
John Tyler (1790–1862), President 1841–45.	There are 8 volumes in the Library of Congress, and a smaller collection in the Duke University Libraries. The University of Virginia Library, William & Mary, College, and the Pierpont Morgan Library have collections ranging up to 130 pieces.	While a large part of the Tyler cache was burned in 1965 when Richmond was put to the torch, the Library of Congress purchased its collection from Tyler's son in 1919 for $1,000.	
James K. Polk (1795–1849), President 1845–49.	The Library of Congress has 188 volumes and boxes. The diary, running to 25 volumes of up to 200 pages each, is in the Chicago Historical Society. Scattered correspondence and papers are in the William L. Clements Library and the Tennessee Historical Society.	There were 2 purchases of Polk papers by the Library of Congress, 1 from a family heir and 1 from the Chicago Historical Society, both of which totaled $13,500.	Y
Zachery Taylor (1784–1850), President 1848–50.	1 volume and 2 boxes are in the Library of Congress. The Kentucky Historical Society (Frankfort), the University of Kentucky Library and the University of North Carolina Library have assorted papers, mostly pre-Presidential.		
Millard Fillmore (1800–74), President 1850–53.	The Buffalo Historical Society has all but a few that are in the Library of Congress.		X
Franklin Pierce (1804–69), President 1853–57.	The largest collection, 1,500 items is in the New Hampshire Historical Society. The Library of Congress has a few additional pieces. But the papers relating to the period of the presidency have, for the most part, disappeared.	Pierce is thought to have destroyed many of his papers; much of his official and personal White House correspondence has disappeared.	
James Buchanan (1791–1868), President 1857–61.	The Library of Congress has 11 volumes and boxes, and the Historical Society of Pennsylvania has 25,000 items. There is a considerable collection in the Lancaster County (Pa.) Historical Society. Smaller collections are in Franklin & Marshall College Library, Dickinson College Library, the Rutherford B. Hayes Library (Freemont, Ohio), the Pierpont Morgan Library, the New York Historical Society, and the Princeton University Library.		X

See footnotes at end of table.

Table 5 Continued

President	Depositories [1]	Purchases [2]
Abraham Lincoln (1809–65), President 1861–65.	The major collection, over 100 volumes and boxes, is in the Library of Congress. The Illinois Historical Society has over 6,000 items. and the Brown University Library 1,678 pieces. There are 4 boxes of material at the University of Chicago. Other collections are at the Chicago Historical Society (50 items), Indiana University Library (215 items), Boston University Libraries (60 items), Harvard College Library (40 items), New York Historical Society (4 volumes and boxes), New York Public Library (4 boxes), Minnesota Historical Society (11 items), Missouri Historical Society (41 items), the Pierpont Morgan Library (26 items), the Rutherford B. Hayes Library (Fremont, Ohio), and Lincoln Memorial University 'Harrogate, Tenn.).	
Andrew Johnson (1808–75), President 1865–69.	The Library of Congress has 275 volumes and boxes. The Rutherford B. Hayes Library has 158 items, and the Duke University Libraries have 42 items.	The Library of Congress acquired its collection of Johnson papers through two purchases from family heirs for $7,500. Y
Ulysses S. Grant (1822–85), President 1869–77.	The Library of Congress has over 100 volumes and boxes. The Henry E. Huntington Library has 345 items, and the Rutherford B. Hayes Library 255 items. Smaller collections are at the Chicago Historical Society (125 pieces), Illinois State Historical Library (200 pieces), Chicago Public Library (10 pieces), Illinois Historical Society (27 letters), the New York Historical Society (35 items), and the Pierpont Morgan Library (11 pieces).	Though not a prolific letter writer, Grant is reported to have returned certain letters he received as Presidentjto the originator of the correspondence. Y
Rutherford B. Hayes (1822–93), President 1877–81.	Some 300 volumes and 75,000 items are in the Rutherford B. Hayes Library in Fremont, Ohio, Hayes's home. Western Reserve University Library has 8 boxes, and the Library of Congress has 5 boxes.	The first actual Presidential library, the Hayes Memorial Library is maintained by the State of Ohio and the Rutherford B. Hayes-Lucy Webb Hayes Foundation. X
James A. Garfield (1831–81), President 1881.	There are 343 volumes and boxes, most pre-Presidential, in the Library of Congress. The Ohio Historical Society has 1 box, and the Rutherford B. Hayes Library has 30 items.	The Library of Congress was made a gift of its Garfield collection in 1930–31 by the former President's children.
Chester A. Arthur (1830–86); President 1881–85.	The Library of Congress has 5 boxes; the New York Historical Society 8 volumes of letters and a box of other papers. The Rutherford B. Hayes Library has 16 items.	
Grover Cleveland (1837–1908).	The major collections are at the Library of Congress with 407 volumes and 109 boxes and the Detroit Public Library with 1,250 items largely relating to the second administration. The Buffalo Historical Society has 75 items, New York Historical Society 30 items, and Pierpont Morgan Library 14 pieces. Princeton University Library also has a varied collection.	The Cleveland collection of the Library of Congress was presented as a gift by Mrs. Preston, the former President's widow
Benjamin Harrison (1833–1901), President 1889–93.	The Library of Congress has 290 volumes and 193 boxes. Indiana Library has a box of papers, and the Rutherford B. Hayes Library 42 items.	The Harrison papers were presented to the Library of Congress by members of the former President's family.
William McKinley (1843–1901), President 1897–1901.	There is a collection of 417 volumes and boxes in the Library of Congress, and other sizable collections are at the Western Reserve Historical Society and the Western Reserve University Library (2 volumes of letters). A few papers are at the Rutherford B. Hayes Library	Approximately 122,000 items were presented to the Library of Congress in 1935 by George B. Cortelyou. the President's personal secretary and executor.
Theodore Roosevelt (1858–1919), President 1901–09.	The Library of Congress has well over 1,000 volumes and boxes. There is another large collection at the Harvard College Library. The Pierpont Morgan Library has the manuscript of his autobiography and some letters. William L. Clements Library has 290 items, the University of Southern California Library 60 items, Bowdoin College Library 15 items, Duke University Libraries 43 pieces, and Yale University Library assorted letters.	The T. R. collection held by the Library of Congress was donated by the former President himself.
William H. Taft (1856–1924), President 1909–13.	There are 1,300 boxes at the Library of Congress. Other collections are at the Yale University Library, Princeton University Library, Western Reserve University Library, and the Ohio Historical Society.	Of the half a million item held by the Library of Congress, none could be consulted prior to 1960 without the consent of the Taft family. The first L. C. deposit of Taft papers was made in 1919 and various additions followed after that time.

See footnotes at end of table.

Table 5 Continued

President	Depositories [1]	Purchases [2]
Woodrow Wilson (1856–1924), President 1913–21.	The Library of Congress has 1,325 boxes. Yale University Library has the Wilson-House correspondence. Harvard College Library has the letters to Walter Hines Page. There are major materials at Princeton University Library and 1,150 items at Columbia University Library. The University of Virginia Library has 248 pieces, the Historical Society of Wisconsin 30 items, the Maryland Historical Society 12 items, and the Woodrow Wilson Foundation has some materials.	The Library of Congress holds the former President's collection of academic materials and certain of his university documents and office items.
Warren G. Harding (1865–1923), President 1921–23.	There are 4 boxes in the Library of Congress, 2 boxes in the Ohio Historical Society and an undisclosed amount in the Harding Memorial Association, Marion, Ohio.	Certain items in the Harding collection will remain under seal until 2014.
Calvin Coolidge (1872–1933), President 1923–29.	The Library of Congress has 347 boxes, and the Forbes Library, Northampton, Mass., 79 volumes and boxes. Smaller collections are at Amherst College Library, the State Library of Massachusetts, and Tulane University Library.	

X

[1] Information regarding papers depositories is generally drawn from Arthur Bernon Tourtellot. The Presidents on the presidency. Garden City, N.Y., Doubleday & Co., 1964, pp. 471–485; updating material supplied by the National Archives and Records Service.

[2] Information regarding purchases of Presidential papers is drawn from David Demarest Lloyd. Presidential papers and Presidential libraries. Manuscripts, v. 8, fall, 1955: 9–15.

Source: Harold C. Relyea, analyst, American National Government, Government and General Research Division, Sept. 24, 1974.

Source: U.S., Congress, House, Committee on House Administration, *The "Public Documents Act" Hearings on H.R. 16902 and Related Legislation.*: 93d Cong., 2d sess., 1974, pp. 245–248.

X indicates the libraries for which descriptions have been provided.

Y indicates the libraries for which some supplementary data have been provided.

Table 6
Presidential Papers in the Library of Congress (Principal Accessions)

President	Date of acquisition by Government (if prior to acquisition by Library)	Mode of Acquisition	Date of acquisition by Library of Congress
Washington	1834-6	.Purchase (family)	1903
	1849	do	1903
Jefferson.	1848	.do	1903
Madison	1837	.do	1903
	1848	do	1903
		Purchase (collector)	1910
Monroe	1849	.Purchase (family)	1903
		do	1950
Jackson.		.Gift (associate's family)	1903
		Purchase (family)	1911
		Purchase (dealer)	1931
Van Buren		.Gift (family)	1904
W. H. Harrison		.do	1933
Tyler		.Purchase (family)	1919
Polk		.do	1903
		Purchase (Historical Society)	1911
Taylor		.Gift (family)	1952
Pierce		.Purchase (family)	1905
Lincoln.		.Gift (family)	1923
Andrew Johnson		.Purchase (family)	1904
		do	1930
Grant		.Gift (family)	1921
		do	1953
		do	1957
Garfield		.do	1921
		do	1963
Arthur		.Purchase (family)	1958
		Gift (family friend)	1971
		Bequest (family)	1972
Cleveland.		.Gift (family)	1928

111

Table 6 Continued

PRESIDENTIAL PAPERS IN THE LIBRARY OF CONGRESS (PRINCIPAL ACCESSIONS)

President	Date of acquisition by Government (if prior to acquisition by Library	Mode of Acquisition	Date of acquisition b Library of Congress
Benjamin Harrison.	.Gift (family)		1933
McKinley	.Gift (executor)[1]		1935
T. Roosevelt	.Gift (president)		1917
	Gift (family)		1919
	do		1922
Taft	.Gift (family)		1952
Wilson	.do[1]		1954
Coolidge	.do[1]		1952

[1]These papers were on deposit at the Library of Congress a number of years before the gift was formalized.
Source: U.S. Congress, House, Committee on House Administration, *"The Public Documents Act": Hearings on H.R. 19602 and Related Legislation*, 93d Cong., 2d sess., 1974, p. 90.

lowed the indexes to the Abraham Lincoln and William Henry Harrison papers. More indexes followed at irregular intervals. By August 1965, seven years after the work had started, sixteen of the twenty-three collections had been indexed and filmed. The three largest collections, all dating from the twentieth century, required the greatest effort. Together these three collections—the papers of Theodore Roosevelt, William Howard Taft, and Woodrow Wilson—contain more than half the presidential paper holdings of the Library of Congress. These sets required multivolume indexes. The Roosevelt index, published in 1970, consists of three volumes; the Taft index, published in 1972, consists of six volumes; and the Wilson index, published in 1973, consists of three volumes.

In all, more than 3,000 reels of microfilm, representing more than 2 million presidential papers, have been produced. The microfilms may be obtained from the Library of Congress by purchase or loan. At least one complete set of the microfilms is held in all states but three. In addition, some other libraries hold substantial portions of the complete set.

Table 7 shows the number of reels produced for each of the twenty-three presidents, the bulk of whose papers are held by the Library of Congress.

After the filming and indexing of the presidential papers was completed, the Library of Congress continued to receive individual manuscripts or small groups of papers for some of the presidential collections. These papers are not part of the Congress-authorized program, but the Library of Congress has issued from time to time supplementary film editions of these additional papers and has made them available in the same way as the components of the basic Congress-authorized presidential papers program.

Some presidential letters and other documents of certain presidents may be found outside the collections devoted to them. The Library of Congress collection of the Benjamin Franklin papers (reproduced on twelve reels of microfilm) contains letters of George Washington, John Adams, and Thomas Jefferson. Similarly, the papers of Nelson Aldrich (reproduced on seventy-three reels of microfilm) include correspondence with Theodore Roosevelt and William Howard Taft.

The index volumes are of great reference value. In addition to the index, the volumes have an introduction, which includes a section on provenance explaining how a collection of presidential papers was formed and how and when the Library of Congress acquired the materials. It also notes other collections in the Library of Congress (collections not part of the microfilmed units) with papers from and to a particular president. Finally, reference is made to other depositories that house additional presidential materials.

The introductory statement includes a description of papers in microfilm. It indicates, for example, that the arrangement is by series, and it lists the items contained in each series. The introduction usually also has a selected bibliography.

The Library of Congress holds the bulk of the papers of twenty-three presidents preceding the Hoover presidency. For these collections, the Library of Congress has issued indexes that also contain historical and provenance information. The Library of Congress does not hold the bulk of the papers of the following presidents: John Adams, John Quincy Adams, Millard Fillmore, John Buchanan, Rutherford B. Hayes, and Warren G. Harding. Since the Library of

Table 7
Microfilm Available for Papers Held by the Library of Congress

PRESIDENT	REELS
Arthur	3
Cleveland	164
Coolidge	190
Garfield	177
Grant	32
B. Harrison	151
W. H. Harrison	3
Jackson	78
Jefferson	65
Johnson	55
Lincoln	97
Madison	28
McKinley	98
Monroe	11
Pierce	7
Polk	67
T. Roosevelt	485
Taft	658
Taylor	2
Tyler	3
Wilson	540
Van Buren	35
Washington	124

Source: U.S., Library of Congress, Manuscript Division, *The Presidential Papers Program of the Library of Congress* (Washington: Library of Congress, n.d.).

Congress was not the major depository for the papers of these presidents, it did not prepare indexes and guides to these papers.

I therefore considered it desirable to seek supporting data for preparing descriptions of these collections of papers. I submitted questionnaires to the librarians or other individuals in charge of the collections for which the Library of Congress is not the principal depository. The questionnaires were similar to those addressed to the libraries in the presidential libraries system, omitting topics applicable only to the federally supported system. Responses were received from all institutions.

In this group is the Rutherford B. Hayes Library, created before the presidential libraries system was established. It is the first presidential library but has remained outside the federally managed system. The Hayes Library has many features in common with the federally supported presidential libraries. It will be at the head of the pre-Hoover collections for which the Library of Congress is not the principal depository. The other collections will be arranged in chronological sequence.

RUTHERFORD B. HAYES LIBRARY

The Rutherford B. Hayes Library, located at Spiegel Grove, Fremont, Ohio, differs in an important aspect from the other presidential libraries. It is not part of the federally supported and administered presidential libraries system. The Hayes Library came into being before the Franklin D. Roosevelt Library—the first federally administered library—was established. This feature of the Hayes Library was emphasized by Thomas A. Smith, who gave an article describing the Hayes Library the title "Before Hyde Park."[10]

The library is affiliated with the Ohio Historical Society but has maintained its independence by being governed by its own board of trustees.

The library's origins date back to March 1910 when the Hayes family deeded Spiegel Grove to the state of Ohio. The transaction was handled by Webb C. Hayes, the president's second son. It was specified in the transaction that the state would erect a fireproof building that would serve as a library and museum. The building was to house the president's papers, his personal effects, and his books. The building was dedicated on Memorial Day 1916. An annex that doubled the capacity was dedicated on October 4, 1922, the hundredth anniversary of Hayes's birth. Subsequently the building was enlarged by east and west wings.

The building that houses the Hayes Center Library and the museum has 54,167 square feet, of which 17,280 square feet are dedicated to storage of books, periodicals, and other library material. This building also contains the library's reading room, administrative offices, an auditorium, two floors of museum exhibits, and conservation and photographic laboratories.

In addition to the library-museum building, the site includes the Hayes residence, the tomb of Rutherford B. and Lucy Hayes, and the restored nineteenth-century Dillon house, built in 1873 for Mr. and Mrs. Charles Dillon, the first neighbors of the Hayes family.[11] The Dillon house is available to overnight guests doing research in the library. Both the Hayes residence and the Dillon house contain artifacts on display and in storage.

The materials included in the collection reflect a career that covers many fields of public life. In addition to being president (1877–1881), Hayes was a city solicitor of Cincinnati, three-term Ohio governor, and a well-known criminal lawyer.

The library has a collection of over 1 million pieces of manuscript. The library director estimates the figure to be greater, but there is no exact count. The director considers it more useful to report that the manuscript collection takes up 2,400 linear feet and that it is growing. Besides the president's papers, there are the papers of his wife, Lucy Webb Hayes, and their children, and papers of presidential advisers and cabinet members. The library includes a number of major collections, such as the papers of Benson Loring, Thomas Nash, John Sherman, William T. Sherman, and William Evart.[12]

The library has prepared guides to facilitate use of the collection, among them an index to the president's personal correspondence and item-by-item indexes for more than 77,000 manuscripts making up the papers of Lucy Webb Hayes and the Hayes children.

The library's photographic collection contains in excess of 50,000 negatives according to the most recent estimate.[13]

The book collection contains about 70,000 bound volumes.[14] The collection emphasizes the latter half of the nineteenth and the early twentieth century. It is particularly strong in Civil War and Reconstruction, the Spanish-American War, local history, civil service, monetary and prison reform, and American Indians. There are special collections included in the book holdings, for instance, the William Dean Howells Collection. The books are classified by the Library of Congress classification scheme.

The library has about 10,000 museum objects. The museum items mirror contemporaneous events, fashion, and tastes. Included are a Victorian parlor in the Hayes residence, the sturdy yet delicately built White House carriage, and a Civil War exhibit. The Dillon house gives a view into an era of elegance and high craftsmanship.[15]

The library still acquires books and other materials of the Gilded

Age period (1865–1916). It is particularly interested in obtaining manuscripts of individuals associated with the federal government during the Hayes presidency.

The papers have been microfilmed and are available on interlibrary loan. They can also be purchased from the Hayes Presidential Center. About a dozen libraries in the United States and in England have purchased the microfilm.

The library is open to the public. The yearly attendance for 1984 was 37,738.

Staff consists of sixteen full-time and eighteen part-time staff members; nine of the full-time staff and seven of the part-time staff are in the professional category. Seven full-time and eleven part-time employees are nonprofessional.

The total annual budget during the years 1983 to 1985 ranged from $694,000 (1983), to $725,000 (1984) to $755,000 (1985 estimated). Twenty-three percent of the funds are from the state of Ohio and 77 percent from private sources. The figures are not precise because of differences in fiscal years between the Hayes Presidential Center and the Ohio Historical Society.

The Hayes Presidential Center publishes a periodical, *The Statesman*, and pamphlets describing the facilities and activities of the center.

From time to time the center offers lectures and film showings. A film series examining the presidency was presented in February 1985. In 1983, the center hosted a symposium on politics in the Gilded Age. In conjunction with the National archives, the center celebrated the one-hundredth anniversary of the passage of the Civil Service Act. Symposium participants were five university professors and a former civil service commissioner. Another participant in the celebrations was Richard Henzel, who played Mark Twain.

JOHN ADAMS AND JOHN QUINCY ADAMS PAPERS

The Adams Papers Collection in the *Massachusetts Historical Society*, Boston, includes the papers of John Adams and John Quincy Adams. The papers occupy about 90 feet of correspondence, diaries, and letter books. Of these items, about 20 percent were sent and received during the presidency, about 50 percent before the presidency, and about 30 percent after the presidency.

Celeste Walker, assistant editor of the Adams papers, notes that the diaries and letter books of John Adams and John Quincy Adams are by nature separate; however, their correspondence and loose papers are interfiled chronologically with those of the rest of the family up to 1890. Figures are estimates. Neither a page count of the loose papers nor a count of their correspondence is available. Walker could, however, provide this more specific information on the manuscript volumes:

| John Adams | Diary 1755–1804): 51 pieces, including stitched and unstitched small paper books. Autobiography (to 1780): 450 pages in three main parts. Letter books: 36. Miscellany volumes: 23. |
| John Quincy Adams | Diary (1779–1848): 50 volumes (assorted sizes and formats). Letter books: 31. Miscellany volumes: 71. |

The Adams family manuscripts that were given to the Massachusetts Historical Society in 1956 have been microfilmed. The 680-reel set can be consulted on the premises of the Massachusetts Historical Society. The set can also be purchased and so far has been acquired by eighty-five libraries throughout the United States and abroad. At these locations, the microfilm collection is also available for use. This microfilm edition is limited to the holdings of the Massachusetts Historical Society.

John Adams's library is in the Boston Public Library. John Quincy Adams's library is in the Boston Athenaeum and the Stone Library of the Adams National Historic Site, Quincy, Massachusetts.

The Adams papers project has accessioned over 26,000 items of Adams material from over 200 repositories. Figures for the individual Adams family members are not available, but the bulk of the materials are the John Adams and John Quincy Adams papers. Repositories with the largest amounts of Adams materials in their various collections are the Library of Congress; the National Archives; the Massachusetts Historical Society (other than the Adams Papers); Houghton Library, Harvard University; the New York Historical Society; Princeton University; the Historical Society of Pennsylvania; and the American Philosophical Society.[16]

MILLARD FILLMORE PAPERS

For a long time it was believed that the Millard Fillmore papers had been destroyed as directed by his son, Millard Powers Fillmore. In 1909, however, forty-four volumes of Millard Fillmore's letter books containing 8,436 letters were found in the attic of Charles D. Marshall, a Buffalo attorney who was the last surviving executor of the estate of Powers Fillmore. After Marshall's death, his daughter deposited the papers in the archives of the Buffalo and Erie County Historical Society, Buffalo, New York. The discovery and deposit of the papers was widely reported in the local press, as well as in the *New York Times Saturday Review of Books*.

These letters represent the bulk of the Fillmore collection of the historical society. However, before as well as after the discovery of the letter books, the society made an effort to obtain Fillmore papers and through its secretary combed the libraries in the hope of finding extant Fillmore items.

The historical society holds, in addition to the letter books, 1 foot of originals and 15.5 feet of photocopies.

Items produced before the presidency consist of approximately 24 feet, and items produced after the presidency consist of approximately 20 feet. Also in the historical society collection are three photographs, three oils, five lithographs, and two paintings of Abigail Fillmore, his first wife, three of Caroline Fillmore, his second wife, and two of Mary Abigail Fillmore, his daughter.

The historical Society has a collection of 550 books, many of them donations of Millard Fillmore and of the second Mrs. Fillmore. In the collection are three catalogs of books and pamphlets. On the basis of these data, it should be possible to reconstruct the library as it existed when the catalogs were completed.

Another major collection of Fillmore papers is held by the State University of New York College of Oswego. The discovery of the Oswego papers was even more remarkable than the discovery in 1909 of the forty-four letter books held at Buffalo. The Oswego papers were found in a home bequeathed to the college. The home came into the possession of the college in 1966, and upon examination of the home's contents, a substantial collection of Fillmore papers came to light. The Buffalo collection is concentrated on the years of Fillmore's presidency, from 1849 to 1853; the Oswego collection touches all other periods of Fillmore's life, from young manhood to death.

The Oswego collection contains material relating to Fillmore's political and social career. It also includes some correspondence between members of the immediate family.

The microfilm edition is the result of a project designed to collect and reproduce as complete a record as attainable of Millard Fillmore's correspondence (letters to and from him), as well as his other writings.[17] Great efforts were made to obtain originals held anywhere in the United States by other repositories and to secure permission to reproduce these originals.

The project was made possible by a grant from the National Historical Publications Commission. The extent of this undertaking becomes obvious as we learn of the many sources consulted. In the National Archives, five different record groups were searched for Fillmore items. In the Library of Congress, about sixty collections were examined with the purpose of finding Fillmore papers. The editors of the microfilm edition also enlisted the cooperation of over one-hundred historical societies, universities, colleges, public libraries, and special libraries in their search for Fillmore papers. Also, individuals and organizations were approached for help, and twelve of this group provided pertinent materials.

When the microfilm edition was prepared, the Oswego collection was interfiled with the Buffalo Historical Society materials, as were the materials from all other sources. The materials are arranged chronologically. Undated materials are arranged alphabetically at end of roll 54.

The microfilm edition is available as a complete set of sixty-eight rolls. Individual rolls may also be purchased separately. The films are distributed by the Buffalo and Erie County Historical Society.

The Buffalo and Erie County Historical Society is open to visitors; however, the original papers are available to neither the general public nor researchers. Microfilm copies may be consulted freely. Although exact statistics are not available, there have been few users. In recent years, there have been few additions only to the collection, and no budget for acquisition purposes is provided.

JAMES BUCHANAN PAPERS

The Buchanan collection held by the Historical Society of Pennsylvania, Philadelphia, is estimated at 25,000 items. Theresa Snyder of the society notes that the staff usually gives an estimate of three pages per letter/item, although some letters are shorter and some longer. The staff knows that the number of pages is at least 25,000 and may be as high as 75,000 pages. Nearly 314 of the papers were produced before the presidency, somewhat less than a fourth during the presidency, and the remainder after the presidency.

The society's *Guide to the Manuscripts Collection* describes in some detail the holdings in entries 91 to 94. The papers deal with all aspects of Buchanan's career. They include letters, reports, and documents of his ministry to Russia and his ministry to England, speeches and notes, miscellaneous correspondence, legal correspondence, business letters, biographical notes and papers on the life of Buchanan, invitations to dinners and public affairs, letters to and from associates, and miscellaneous letters of the Buchanan family.

The collection includes some portraits and other photographs, arranged within the print collection.

The microfilm set comprises sixty reels. Reels may be consulted on the society's premises and may be borrowed on interlibrary loan. The microfilm edition may be purchased through University Microfilms International.

Access to the original papers is restricted; however, the chief of manuscripts may give access at his discretion. The society encourages the use of the microfilm.

WARREN G. HARDING PAPERS

The Ohio Historical Society, Columbus, Ohio, is the principal repository of the papers of President Warren Gamaliel Harding. The papers originating in the White House and received by the White House during Harding's presidency were assigned to either of two files: the Official File and the Private File. All mail was received in the executive wing. The items intended for Harding's private attention were routed to his private office and filed there. The same scheme of filing was applied to both files, but much more care was given to the arrangement of the official material.

After Harding's death on August 2, 1923, all papers should have been removed from the White House. But instead of sending all papers to Ohio, Harding's secretary, George B. Christian, Jr., shipped only the private papers there and stored the official papers in the White House basement.

Mrs. Harding reserved for herself the right to examine private papers with the intention of destroying those that in her view might be harmful to her husband's memory. It is believed that Mrs. Harding not only went through the private White House file but also through the papers left in Marion in the offices of the *Marion Star*, with which Harding had been affiliated as editor and in other capacities.

Mrs. Harding died on November 21, 1924. In her will, she left her own papers and those of her husband to the newly formed Harding Memorial Association. For this reason, the official papers, stored in the White House basement and discovered in 1929 by workmen, became part of Mrs. Harding's estate and were sent to the Harding Memorial Association at Marion. The official papers were in good shape, practically complete, and still arranged in their original sequence.

On October 3, 1963, the Harding papers in the possession of the Harding Memorial Association were donated to the Ohio Historical Society. They were opened to the public on April 25, 1964. Additions to this gift were made through 1964 and 1965.

The Harding papers consist of 907 document boxes, occupying 226 linear feet and numbering approximately 350,000 items. A grant of $40,000 from the National Historical Publications Commission enabled the Harding papers to be microfilmed. The microfilm edition consists of 263 rolls with 356,827 exposures and an average number of 1,357 exposures per roll.[18]

The microfilm edition of the Harding papers is divided into twenty series.[19] The first six series include all Harding papers, followed by seven series of related collections. The remaining seven series are not part of the major Harding collections but are separate collections of the society. They may be conveniently divided into these segments:

Marion papers (1888–1920) rolls 1–19: They include all materials dealing with Harding until his election as a senator in 1914 and all papers subsequently deposited at Marion until 1920, with the exception of those shipped to Washington at Harding's request.

Senatorial papers (1915–1921), rolls 20–27.

Presidential election papers (1918–1921), rolls 28–129.

Presidential papers (1921–1923), rolls 130–237.

Remaining rolls, 238–263: contain speeches by Harding delivered between 1899 and 1923; Harding papers acquired independently of the Harding Memorial Association; genealogical data; Florence Harding Papers; Harding Memorial Association papers and collections of Harding materials assembled by George B. Christian, Sr., George B. Christian, Jr., Cyril Clemens, Ray Baker Harris, and others.

The Warren G. Harding Papers: An Inventory to the Microfilm Edition gives for each of the 263 rolls a detailed contents note and also refers to the boxes in which the original materials corresponding to the films are kept. The publication carries conversion tables necessary for the validation of references to papers made prior to the organization for the microfilm edition.[20] Among other useful information, there is a guide to related materials in the Ohio Historical Society and in other repositories.[21]

In addition to the Harding papers and the related papers included in the microfilm edition, the Ohio Historical Society possesses collections of political figures active during Harding's presidency or even involved with him. Outstanding among these are the papers of Harry M. Daugherty, his attorney general. Also important for research in the Harding area are the complete files of the *Marion Star* and other Ohio newspapers.

The Ohio Historical Society further holds Harding's personal library of 1,917 titles, as well as a number of works (books, pamphlets, periodicals) relating to Harding. These have been classified in accordance with the Dewey classification scheme.

The Ohio Historical Society has a number of audiovisual items, none included in the microfilm edition.

A video collection consisting of eight reels of 16 mm acetate positive film is arranged in random order. The original collection consisted of twenty-two nitrate films that were deteriorating and were restored by change to acetate.

There are a collection of twelve print portraits of Harding by various artists and thirty-six boxes of photographs, cartoons, and other items. The photographs deal mostly with Harding's career. The items occupy 24 linear feet.[22]

The Harding papers are handled by the Ohio Historical Society staff. No staff member is exclusively assigned to the care of Harding materials. The entire Harding collection is open to all researchers. The original manuscript collection and the microfilm collection may be used in the reading room. Researchers may obtain microfilm copies on interlibrary loan from the Ohio Historical Society or from institutions that have acquired the microfilm edition. Part or all of the microfilm edition may be purchased from the society.[23]

The Harding home and the Harding tomb are among the sites operated by the Ohio Historical Society.[24] Some artifacts are displayed at the home. Periodically the society sponsors events such as an exhibit on political memorabilia entitled "Banners, Buttons, and Broadsides," which opened at the society on October 7, 1984. There was a reenactment of Harding's "front porch" campaign at the Harding home.[25]

ADDITIONAL DATA FOR SEVERAL COLLECTIONS

There are a number of active publication projects, supported by the National Historical Publications Commission, dealing with the papers of several presidents, the bulk of whose papers is held by the Library of Congress. The projects concern the papers of George Washington, Thomas Jefferson, James Madison, Andrew Jackson, James K. Polk, Andrew Johnson, Ulysses P. Grant, and Woodrow Wilson.

I sent to each of the editors the pertinent holdings statement from table 5 and asked them to suggest any necessary additions, deletions, or other changes. Their responses appear as notes arranged in chronological sequence. On table 5, the eight entries for which additional data have been provided are labeled by the letter Y.

Several respondents suggested that a more complete picture of the holdings would be obtained by a search for papers in the National Archives.

George Washington Papers

Dorothy Twohig, associate editor of the papers of George Washington, stated in a letter dated November 22, 1985, that she and her associates would not be able to provide information since the collecting and cataloging of their Washington materials—so far 125,000 copies of documents—had been undertaken before information was controlled by computers. If computers had been applied, pertinent information could have been extracted.

Thomas Jefferson Papers

Charles T. Cullen, editor of the papers of Thomas Jefferson, considers the description of the collections accurate. He observes that no caches of documents have appeared or been acquired by anyone during the past decade.

The number of Jefferson documents owned by Princeton is 200. In table 5, a reference was made to American Philosophic Society; it should have read Philosophical Society.

James Madison Papers

The editor of the James Madison papers, Robert A. Rutland, notes in a letter dated October 31, 1985, that the Princeton Library acquired the Jasper Crane collection in the late 1970s and that the Massachusetts Historical Society received the George Cutler collection. Both are relatively large holdings of James Madison papers. He states further that the National Archives holdings are scattered in many record groups, mainly in RG59 (State Department).

Andrew Jackson Papers

The editor of the Andrew Jackson papers, Harold D. Moser, observed in a letter dated November 11, 1985, that in addition to the holdings noted, the National Archives has several thousand items.

James K. Polk Papers

E. Wayne Cutter, editor of the correspondence of James K. Polk, noted that the twenty-five-volume presidential diary is not in the Chicago Historical Society collections but in the Library of Congress.

He believes that in the tabulation, the major and minor collections were correctly listed.

Andrew Johnson Papers

The editor of the papers of Andrew Johnson, LeRoy P. Graf, in a letter dated November 18, 1985, offers the following additions:

Huntington Library, San Marino, California—about forty items.

Pierpont Morgan Library, New York City—eighty items or more.

Margaret Johnson Patterson Bartlett Collection, most of which is now in the library at Tusculum College, Greeneville, Tennessee.

Massachusetts Historical Society, Boston, Massachusetts—forty-one items.

Tennessee State Library and Archives, Nashville, Tennessee.

University of Rochester Library—over ninety items.

Graf emphasizes that in addition, the National Archives has Johnson material scattered in a multitude of record groups. He adds that the editors of the Johnson papers are interested in letters and telegrams to Johnson, as well as from him, so that the figures he supplied incorporate both kinds of items. Where no estimate is given, it is assumed that the number exceeds one hundred and that "we have not filed them in a way that we can recover a more accurate figure for you."

Ulysses S. Grant Papers

The editor of the papers of Ulysses S. Grant, John Y. Simon, by letter dated December 17, 1985, questions why there is an entry for the Illinois State Historical Society and another for the Illinois Historical Society. He also considers the comment about Grant's returning correspondence "rather misleading." He further notes that the holdings of the National Archives should be taken into account.

Woodrow Wilson Papers

The editor of the papers of Woodrow Wilson, Arthur S. Link, suggested in a letter dated July 1, 1985, that the present notation regarding holdings by the Princeton University be replaced by the following: "The second largest collection is the Woodrow Wilson collection in the Princeton University Library."

NOTES

1. Rowland Buford, "The Papers of the Presidents," *American Archivist* 13, no. 3 (July 1950): 195–211.

2. Arnold Hirshon, "The Scope, Accessibility and History of Presidential Papers," *Government Publications Review* 1, no. 4 (Fall 1974): 363–90. See especially pp. 377–90, containing a chronological history of the papers of the presidents after they left office.

3. "Résumé of Presidential Papers," in U.S. Congress, House, Committee on Government Operations, *To Provide for the Acceptance and Maintenance of Presidential Libraries, and for Other Purposes: Hearing on H.J. Res. 330, H.J. Res. 331 and H.J. Res. 332,* 84th Cong. 1st sess., 1955, pp. 39–44.

4. "Depositories and Purchases of Presidential Papers," in U.S. Congress, House, Committee on House Administration, *The "Public Documents Act": Hearings on H.R. 16902 and Related Legislation,* 93d Cong., 2d sess., 1974, appendix 1.

5. Harold C. Relyea, Letter to author, April 17, 1985.

6. *"Public Documents Act,"* p. 91.

7. The six presidents whose principal holdings are not in the Library of Congress are John Adams, John Quincy Adams, John Buchanan, Millard Fillmore, Rutherford B. Hayes, and Warren G. Harding.

8. *"Public Documents Act,"* p. 88.

9. The discussion of the program is based on U.S. Library of Congress, *The Presidential Papers Program of the Library of Congress, Manuscript Division* (Washington, n.d.).

10. Thomas A. Smith, "Before Hyde Park: The Rutherford B. Hayes Library," *American Archivist* 43, no. 4 (Fall 1980): 485–88. This article is one of my principal sources. Other data were obtained by questionnaire, supplemented by letters from Leslie H. Fishel, Jr., director of the Rutherford B. Hayes Presidential Center.

11. Rutherford B. Hayes Presidential Center, [description of center] folder, illustrated; Rutherford B. Hayes Presidential Center, *The Dillon House* (n.d.).

12. Leslie H. Fishel, Jr., Letter to author, January 2, 1986.

13. This is a revised figure. Ibid.

14. This is a revised figure. Based on a shelf list inventory, the stated holdings were reduced from 100,000 to 60,000. A review, including acquisitions since the shelf list inventory, has resulted in a reliable rounded figure of 70,000. Ibid.

15. Article heading in Dillon house folder.

16. Based on information supplied by John D. Cushing, librarian, Massachusetts Historical Society, supplemented by Celeste Walker, assistant editor, Adams Papers, her letter to author, January 15, 1986.

17. *Guide to the Microfilm Edition of the Millard Fillmore Papers,* esp. pp. 2–11, 17, 27.

18. Andrea D. Lentz, *The Warren G. Harding Papers: An Inventory to the Microfilm Edition* (Columbus, Ohio: Ohio Historical Society, Archives

and Manuscripts Division, 1970), Introduction and Provenance (pp. 3–10); Note to Researchers (pp. 1–2).

19. Ibid., pp. 13–16.

20. Ibid., pp. 116–35.

21. Ibid., pp. 282–83.

22. The items are described on several separate, mimeographed inventory sheets.

23. Lentz, *Warren G. Harding Papers*, p. 1.

24. Ibid., following p. 115 and preceding p. 34. For visitor information regarding home and tomb, consult the society's site directory.

25. Gary J. Arnold, assistant archivist, Archives-Library Division, Letter to author, January 18, 1985.

7

The Future

The increasing cost of maintaining the presidential libraries engendered congressional efforts to reduce such costs. These efforts resulted in the Presidential Libraries Act of 1986, which imposed mandatory endowments. One may speculate as to whether mandatory endowments will be accepted by future presidents and their supporting organizations or whether they will be rejected as too burdensome. Although there is no doubt that the president and his supporting organizations would have preferred to continue the practice of fixing without interference the size and disposition of their contribution, it may still be assumed that they will provide the funds in accordance with the mandatory endowment provisions. If the president and his supporting organizations should not make any contribution to the maintenance of the library, they would probably also be excluded from participating in the planning of a library. It could also be assumed that an archival depository built exclusively with federal funds would be completely utilitarian, highly selective as to acquisitions, and possibly, for lack of space, exclude most museum objects.

During the many discussions relating to cost reduction, there was never any recommendation that the existing presidential libraries be abandoned and new ones no longer established. In all discussions, it was stated or implied that the presidential libraries contain important national assets that must be maintained and protected and made available for use.

It seems certain that technical advances in the communications field will be applied extensively to the operations of presidential libraries. Tests of computer applications have already been undertaken. Their successful completion ensures their gradual introduction into all libraries. Computers will be useful in managerial tasks. More important, computers will facilitate, refine, and, if necessary, individualize the preparation of finding aids. Moreover, networks are envisaged that will connect all presidential libraries. Such networks will make possible the joint use of some of the presidential library resources. Eventually presidential libraries may be connected with other types of libraries, such as academic and research libraries. Information can then flow from these libraries to presidential libraries, and vice-versa.

The presidential libraries have become integral parts of the national political and social fabric. They offer rich historical resources, many unique, and for this reason they appeal to scholars. To the lay public, they show in an attractive setting not only documents and other objects created and received during a president's term of office but also documents and other materials covering his total life span.

Appendix 1

Cost of Presidential
Libraries, FY 1955
through FY 1987

	HOOVER	ROOSEVELT	TRUMAN	EISENHOWER	KENNEDY	JOHNSON	FORD
1955		63,745					
1956		64,853					
1957		70,076	4,760				
1958		81,059	61,477				
1959		87,347	80,710				
1960		91,444	88,696				
1961		105,177	94,601	19,445			
1962	28,678	112,881	94,450	58,288			
1963	42,665	107,866	102,067	72,922			
1964	33,622	105,754	111,077	83,055			
1965	87,314	120,701	121,506	99,432			
1966	90,088	125,209	125,839	94,567			
1967	101,216	114,052	132,359	103,259			
1968	93,000	126,000	140,000	100,000	37,000	86,000	
1969	125,034	162,309	212,117	202,030	104,847	396,585	
1970	183,562	258,325	297,931	296,030	338,312	433,916	
1971	199,387	287,696	318,975	318,948	354,351	554,640	
1972	222,258	315,439	329,270	359,949	434,329	567,877	
1973	228,143	340,105	313,845	383,537	496,673	587,511	
1974	256,912	335,422	327,883	425,475	547,629	612,265	
1975	258,495	400,444	389,338	443,107	561,851	659,709	
1976 & TQ	350,000	586,000	578,000	611,000	760,000	996,000	16,000
1977	309,000	468,000	497,000	514,000	637,000	725,000	352,000
1978	321,000	475,000	463,000	486,000	662,000	713,000	238,000
1979	355,799	523,528	520,012	511,959	702,142	754,556	243,481
1980	388,000	541,000	529,000	512,000	727,000	786,000	447,000
1981	421,000	560,000	569,000	545,000	757,000	782,000	455,000
1982	484,000	536,000	627,000	545,000	831,000	834,000	528,000
1983	516,000	561,000	660,000	600,000	885,000	860,000	572,000
1984	493,000	566,000	719,000	656,000	843,000	891,000	611,000
1985	477,000	569,000	738,000	708,000	870,000	920,000	633,000
1986 EST.	512,000	611,000	792,000	760,000	933,000	988,000	680,000
1987 EST.	515,000	614,000	796,000	765,000	938,000	994,000	684,000

NIXON	CARTER	Sub-Total Program Costs	SLUC and Actual Costs*	Recurring Reimbursable	Library Totals	Central Office**	I	GRAND TOTAL
		63,745			63,745		I	63,745
		64,853			64,853		I	64,853
		74,836			74,836		I	74,836
		142,536			142,536		I	142,536
		168,057			168,057		I	168,057
		180,140			180,140		I	180,140
		219,223			219,223		I	219,223
		294,297			294,297		I	294,297
		325,520			325,520		I	325,520
		333,508			333,508	46,743	I	380,251
		428,953			428,953	130,532	I	559,485
		435,703			435,703	176,263	I	611,966
		450,886			450,886	182,859	I	613,745
		582,000			582,000	91,000	I	673,000
		1,202,922			1,202,922	203,902	I	1,406,824
		1,808,076			1,808,076	172,779	I	1,980,855
47,923		2,081,920			2,081,920	170,369	I	2,252,289
66,155		2,295,277			2,295,277	218,282	I	2,513,559
113,111		2,462,925			2,462,925	259,191	I	2,722,116
109,738		2,615,324			2,615,324	249,133	I	2,863,457
93,850		2,812,844	578,111	808,032	4,198,987	343,460	I	4,542,447
124,000		4,021,000	960,959	1,016,421	5,998,380	583,000	I	6,581,380
111,000		3,613,000	998,825	1,099,786	5,711,611	612,000	I	6,323,611
525,000		3,883,000	1,306,150	1,173,336	6,362,486	868,000	I	7,230,486
619,620		4,231,097	1,302,957	1,212,184	6,746,238	777,545	I	7,523,783
667,000		4,597,000	2,557,000	2,073,000	9,227,000	944,000	I	10,171,000
657,000	762,000	5,508,000	3,341,000	2,477,000	11,326,000	369,000	I	12,295,000
644,000	422,000	5,451,000	4,847,000	434,000	10,732,000	771,000	I	11,503,000
628,000	305,000	5,587,000	5,924,000	466,000	11,977,000	995,000	I	12,972,000
613,000	328,000	5,720,000	6,791,000	72,000	12,583,000	1,767,000	I	14,350,000
706,000	405,000	6,026,000	7,366,000	27,000	13,419,000	1,217,000	I	14,636,000
758,000	434,000	6,468,000	12,128,000	42,000	18,638,000	1,174,000	I	19,812,000
762,000	1,039,000	7,107,000	7,907,000	43,000	15,057,000	1,145,000	I	16,202,000

*In FY 1982, the administrator removed the presidential libraries from the SLUC payments to the federal buildings Fund, and NARS began reimbursing the fund on the basis of actual costs.
**Includes Commmon Distributables.
Note: Costs are in dollars.
Source: Office of Presidential Libraries.

SLUC = Standard Level User Charges
NARS = National Archives and Records Service

Appendix 2

Presidential Libraries Questionnaire

   I. Name of library
  II. Date of founding of library
 III. Kinds of materials in your library*
     1. Papers
       a) Produced during the presidency
       b) Produced before the presidency
       c) Produced after the presidency
     2. Books
     3. Periodicals
     4. Photographs, sound recordings, and other audiovisual media
     5. Museum objects

*For categories listed under III and IV, give number of items. If exact figures are not available, give approximate figures; if figures are not available under the questionnaire categories, list figures—exact or approximate—under your categories.

IV. Does your library include papers from:
1. The presidential family?
2. Presidential advisers?
3. Members of the cabinet in office during the presidency?
4. Other categories?
V. What is your acquisitions policy?
VI. By what scheme do you arrange or classify your materials?
1. Papers. Are the following your main processing categories:
President's own files
White House Central Files
National Security Files
Files of White House Staff Members
If not, what scheme(s) do you use?
2. Books
3. Periodicals
4. Photographs and other audiovisual items
5. Museum objects
6. Were the president's papers arranged or classified while the president was still in office? If so, by whom and to what extent?
VII. Do you intend to microfilm the presidential papers?
1. All
2. Some (give categories)
VIII. How many staff members does your library have in addition to the director?
1. Professional staff
a) Archivists
b) Librarians
c) Other professional staff
2. Nonprofessional staff
a) Technical assistants
b) Clerks
c) Other nonprofessional staff
IX. Use of the library
1. Is the library freely open to the general public? If not, what are the conditions?
2. Is the library freely open to persons engaged in research in the presidential field?
3. Is access to some materials restricted? Give categories and the duration of restricted access for the several categories.
4. Are the museum objects (or most of the museum objects) separately housed? If so, is there a separate entrance to the museum section?

     5. If available, give number of annual visitors. If there is a breakdown by categories, use these subdivisions.

  X. Does the library offer:
    1. Seminars
    2. Institutes
    3. Publications

 XI. Building
    1. Date of opening to the public
    2. Size
    3. Cost
    If available, enclose picture of building and floor plan. Also, describe briefly arrangement of facilities.

XII. Annual budget for last three years (for acquisition, for staff, for other purposes)
Approximately what percentage of your funds is derived from private sources? Are these funds usually earmarked for specific purposes, or is the use of these funds left to the library administration's discretion?

The cover letter accompanying the questionnaire noted: "It would also be helpful if you could send me literature relating to your library, such as articles, pamphlets for users and visitors, reports (annual or special), as well as any other items you deem useful for this project."

Appendix 3

Presidential Libraries' Supporting Organizations

FRANKLIN D. ROOSEVELT LIBRARY

Name and Address of Organization
Franklin D. Roosevelt-Four Freedoms Foundation
c/o New York State Office of Special Projects
4 Burnett Boulevard
Poughkeepsie, New York 12603

Officers
Honorary chairman: W. Averell Harriman
Cochairman: Senator Jonathan Bingham
Cochairman: Arthur Schlesinger, Jr.
President: William J. vanden Heuvel
Executive director: Frederica Goodman

Source: Office of Presidential Libraries, November 1984.

Legal Status
Incorporated in the state of New York as a nonprofit organization.

Purpose
Newly reorganized, this foundation has just established a grant award committee that will recommend grants of up to $2,500 for scholarly research at the library.

Name and Address of Organization
Eleanor Roosevelt Institute
c/o Foundation for Child Development
345 East 46th Street
New York, New York 10017

Officer
Chairman, board of directors: Trude W. Lash

Library Activities
—Supported most of the costs ($85,000) of an oral history program, conducted 1977–1980, aimed at gathering the recollections of Mrs. Roosevelt's friends.
—From 1973 to 1981, supported a small grant-in-aid program for young scholars, which was administered by the library on behalf of the institute. The institute expended between $15,000 and $20,000 annually for this program. In 1981, the institute's board of directors decided to end this program and to use its funds (estimated at $75,000 annually) to support activities directed by itself or done in conjunction with other foundations.

HARRY S. TRUMAN LIBRARY

Name and Address of Organization
Harry S. Truman Library Institute
Apartment 707
121 West 48th Street
Kansas City, Missouri 64112

Officer
President: James C. Olson (president emeritus, University of Missouri)

Legal Status
Established 1957 as a nonprofit corporation.

Purpose
To support the growth of the Truman Library as a major research center.

Activities
—Fund research grants ranging from $1,000 to $10,000.
—Awards a book prize biennially of $5,000 for best book on the
public career of Harry S. Truman or on some aspect of U.S. po-
litical, social, or ecnomic history between 1945 and 1953.
—Sponsors conferences.
—Underwrites a quarterly newsletter, *Whistle Stop*, featuring ar-
ticles on current activities at the Truman Library.
—Has paid for the preparation of two slide shows, totalling $6,000.
—Has purchased books and microfilm publications relevant to Tru-
man and to the institution of the presidency, totaling $12,000.
—Awarded a grant to the Mid-America Arts Alliance to assist the
Truman Library in preparing the 1984 centennial celebration of
Truman's birth, totaling $11,000.

HERBERT HOOVER LIBRARY

Name and Address of Organization
Herbert Hoover Presidential Library Association, Inc.
P.O. Box 696
West Branch, Iowa 52358

Officers
President and Chairman: Richard C. Kautz
Executive director: John T. Fawcett

Legal Status
Incorporated in state of Iowa as a nonprofit educational organization.

Purpose
To help support the Hoover Library as a center for independent
scholarly research dealing with the ideals and personal philosophy
of Herbert Hoover; the accomplishments of Herbert Hoover in the
field of public policy; and the functioning of the American government, insofar as such research is consistent with Hoover's own work
in improving the organization and role of government.

Activities
—Funds annual research grants ranging from $1,000 to $10,000
—Sponsors conferences (most recently, in September 1984, a con-
ference on soil and water conservation, with Senators Roger Jep-
sen and Mark Hatfield as featured speakers).
—Has purchased exhibit cases and library furniture in excess of
$45,000.
—Has awarded a $400,000 commission to a historian for a multi-
volume biography of Herbert Hoover. *The Life of Herbert Hoover:*

The Engineer, 1874–1914, by George H. Nash, is the first volume of that biography, appearing in 1983.

DWIGHT D. EISENHOWER LIBRARY

Name and Address of Organization
Eisenhower Foundation
1112 North Buckeye
Abilene, Kansas 67410

Officers
Chairman of the board: Harry Darby
President: Calvin Strowig

Legal Status
A nonpublic, tax-exempt foundation; membership by invitation only.

Assets

Estimated t $240,000. All is invested; foundation functions from the interest.

Purpose
Originally established in order to honor Eisenhower for his leadership in World War II but grew into an organization that, among other things, assists the work of the library. In fact, the foundation raised funds to build the library and museum buildings.

Activities
—Publishes a quarterly newsletter, *Overview*, featuring articles on the library's activities.
—Provides financial support for conferences and commemorative ceremonies.
—Provides financial support for travel, for the purpose of soliciting manuscripts for the library, and for collecting oral history interviews (average $1,000 annually).

JOHN F. KENNEDY LIBRARY

Name and Address of Organization
John F. Kennedy Library Foundation, Inc.
c/o Cullinet Software
400 Blue Hill Drive
Westwood, MA 02090

Officers
President: John J. Cullinane

Vice-president: Caroline B. Kennedy
Vice-president: Frederick A. Wang

Legal Status
The John F. Kennedy Library Corporation, which built and equipped
the John F. Kennedy Library, was reconstituted in 1984 as the John
F. Kennedy Library Foundation, Incorporated.

Activities
—During its existence, the Kennedy Library Corporation provided
an annual sum of approximately $20,000, which went for the sup-
port of scholarly conferences, miscellaneous entertainment expenses, and small, nonpermanent museum exhibits. In March
1982, the corporation transferred $66,000 to the trust fund to cover
library expenses incurred at that time.
—The Kennedy Library Foundation is engaged in raising an endowment of $8 million, the interest of which will be used for new
museum exhibits, educational programs, a community information program, an audiovisual program for elementary and secondary schools, and other library programs.

LYNDON BAINES JOHNSON LIBRARY

Name and Address of Organization
Lyndon Baines Johnson Foundation
2313 Red River Street
Austin, Texas 78705

Officer
Executive director: Lawrence D. Reed

Legal Status
Incorporated in state of Texas as a nonprofit, charitable, and educational corporation. The division of the foundation that is concerned
with Johnson Library activities is called the Friends of the LBJ
Library.

Activities
—Supports the entire sales desk operation of the library.
—Finances a grant-in-aid program for research.
—Supports the lecture and symposium program.
—Supports the oral history program.
—Publishes a newsletter three times a year, *Among Friends of LBJ*,
featuring articles on activities at the library.

GERALD R. FORD LIBRARY

Name and Address of Organization
Gerald R. Ford Foundation
13999 West Bay Shore Drive
Traverse City, Michigan 49684

Officer
Chairman: Honorable Robert P. Griffin

Legal Status
Established in the state of Michigan as a nonprofit corporation.

Purpose
To support the Ford Library in Ann Arbor, Michigan, and the Ford
Museum in Grand Rapids, Michigan.

Activities
—Awards grants of up to $2,000 for scholarly research at the library.
—Lends support to conferences and symposia at the library (most
  recently, the foundation cosponsored with the library a First Ladies Conference, held at the museum in April 1985).
—Lends support to museum exhibits (for example, the foundation
  commissioned the space-man statue that now stands in the front
  of the museum).
—Publishes *Gerald R. Ford Foundation Newsletter* featuring articles
  on library and museum activities.

JIMMY CARTER LIBRARY

Name and Address of Organization
Carter Presidential Library
c/o Lipshutz, Frankel, Greenblatt, King & Cohen
2300 Harris Tower, Peachtree Center
233 Peachtree Street, Northwest
Atlanta, Georgia 30043

Officer
Treasurer and trustee: Robert J. Lipshutz

Purpose
—Construct and donate a library building.
—Establish, with Emory University, a center for the study of issues
  affecting the public interest.
—Support the library's outreach programs.
—Fund an oral history program.
—Fund the museum's exhibit program.

Bibliography

Berman, Larry. "The Evolution and Value of Presidential Libraries," *in* Harold C. Relyea et al., *The Presidency and Information Policy,* New York: Center for the Study of the Presidency; Proceedings 4, no. 1, 1981, pp. 79–91.

Brooks, Philip C. "Understanding the Presidency: The Harry S. Truman Library," *Prologue* 1, no. 3 (Winter 1969): 3–12.

Buford, Rowland. "The Papers of the Presidentss," *American Archivist* 13, no. 3 (July 1950 : 195–211.

Cappon, Lester J. "Why Presidential Libraries?" *Yale Review* 68, no. 1 (Autumn 1978): 11–13.

Cochrane, James L. "The U.S. Presidential Libraries and the History of Political Economy," *History of Political Economy* 8, no. 3 (Fall 1976): 412–427.

Connor, R.D.W. "The Franklin D. Roosevelt Library," *American Archivist* 3, no. 2 (April 1940): 81–92.

Cook, J. Frank. "Private Papers of Public Officials," *American Archivist* 38, no. 3 (July 1975): 299–324.

Drewry, Elizabeth. "The Role of Presidential Libraries," *Midwest Quarterly* 7, no. 1 (October 1965): 53–65.

Eisenhower, John S.D. "Those Presidential Papers," *New York Times*, January 12, 1975.

Elliott, J.L. *Presidential Papers and the Presidential Library System*, Provo, Utah: Brigham Young University, School of Library and Information Sciences, 1981.

Geselbrecht, Raymond. "The Four Eras in the History of Presidential Papers," *Prologue* 15, no. 1 (Spring 1983): 37–42.

Hirshon, Arnold. "Recent Developments in the Accessibility of Presidential Papers and Other Presidential Historical Materials," *Government Publications Review* 6, no. 4 (1979):343–357.

———. "The Scope, Accessibility and History of Presidential Papers," *Government Publication Review* 1 (Fall 1974): 363–390.

Jones, H. G. "Presidential Libraries: Is There a Case for a National Presidential Library?" *American Archivist* 38, no. 3 (July 1975): 325–328.

———. *The Records of a Nation: Their Management, Preservation and Use.* New York: Atheneum, 1969.

Kahn, Herman. "The Presidential Library—A New Institution," *Special Libraries* 50, no. 3 (March 1959): 106–113.

Leland, Waldo G. "The Creation of the Franklin D. Roosevelt Library: A Personal Narrative," *American Archivist* 18, no. 1 (January 1955): 11–31.

Lloyd, David D. "Presidential Papers and Presidential Libraries," *Manuscripts* 8, no. 1 (Fall 1955): 4–15.

Lovely, Sister Louise. "The Evolution of Presidential Libraries," *Government Publications Review* 6, no. 1 (1979): 27–35.

McCoy, Donald R. *The National Archives: America's Ministry of Documents 1934–1968.* Chapel Hill: University of North Carolina Press, 1978.

McKay, Pamela R."Presidential Papers: A Property Issue," *Library Quarterly* 52, no. 1 (January 1982): 21–40.

Menez, Joseph F. "Presidential Papers and Presidential Libraries," *Social Science* 47, no. 1 (Winter 1972): 34–39.

National Archives and Records Administration. *Presidential Libraries Manual.* Washington: NARA, April 15, 1985 (Libraries 1401).

O'Neill, James E. "Will Success Spoil the Presidential Libraries?" *American Archivist* 36, no. 3 (July 1973): 339–351.

Peace, Nancy E., ed. *Archival Choices: Managing the Historical Record in an Age of Abundance.* Lexington, Mass.: Lexington Books, 1984.

Rhoads, James B. "Who Should Own the Documents of Public Officials?" *Prologue* 7, no. 1 (Spring 1975): 32–35.

Riley, Tom and Relyea, Harold C., editors. *Freedom of Information Trends in the Information Age.* London and Totowa, N.J.: Frank Cass & Co., 1983.

Schlesinger, Arthur, Jr. "Who Owns a President's Papers?" *Wall Street Journal*, February 26, 1975.

Taft, William H. *Our Chief Magistrate and His Powers.* New York: Columbia University Press, 1916.

U.S. Library of Congress. *The Presidential Papers Program of the Library of Congress, Manuscript Division.* Washington, [n.d.].

Wigdor, Alexandra K. and Wigdor, David. "The Future of Presidential Papers," *in* Harold C. Relyea et al., *The Presidency and Information Policy*, New York: Center for the Study of the Presidency; Proceedings 4, no. 1, 1981, pp. 92–101.

Index

Acquisition programs, 46, 49. *See also under individual libraries*

Adams, John, 113, 117–19

Adams, John, Library, in Boston Public Library, 118

Adams, John Quincy, 113, 117–19

Adams, John Quincy, Library, in Boston Athenaeum, 118

Adams, John Quincy, Library, in Stone Library, 118

Adams papers, 117–19

Advisory agencies, records of, 33

Aldrich, Nelson, 113

Ancillary function, 20

Anderson, William J., 22

Archival depositories, patterns of, 31–32

Archivists, assistance by, 53

Arthur, Chester A., 3

Berman, Larry S., 35

Brademas, John, 11

Broderick, Paul L., 106

Buchanan, John, 113, 120–21

Buchanan papers, 113, 120–21

Buford, Rowland, 105

Buildings, 21

Carter, Rosalynn, 99

Carter Presidential Library, 24, 98–101

Carter Presidential Materials Project, 98

Central library, 22–23

Christian, George B., Jr., 121

Citations, forms of, 54–55
Classification system, 32
Cleveland, Grover, 4–5
Colson, Charles, 89
Computer applications, 37–38, 130
Coolidge, Calvin, 4, 106
Copyright protection, 55
Core functions, 26
Cullen, Charles T., 124
Cutter, E. Wayne, 124

Data, interpretation of, 35–36
Daugherty, Harry M., 122
Dean, John, 89
Deeds of gifts, 46
Deitch, Joseph, 37, 39 n.18
Dillon, Charles, 116

Ehrlichman, John, 89
Eisenhower, John S. D., 11
Eisenhower Presidential Library,
    70–75; Britt Brown Small Arms
    Collection, 74; military currency
    collection, 74; *Quarterly List of
    Declassified Documents*, 72
Emerson, William R., 59
Endowments, mandatory, 25, 27–
    28, 129
Evert, William, 116

Fenn, Dan H., 75
Files, 33–34
Fillmore, Millard, 3, 113, 118–20
Fillmore, Millard Powers, 118
Fillmore book collection: Buffalo
    and Erie County Historical Soci-
    ety, 119
Fillmore papers, 118–20; Buffalo
    and Erie County Historical Soci-
    ety, 119; State University of
    New York College of Oswego,
    119, 120
Finding aids, 52
Ford Museum, 93–98
Ford Presidential Library, 93–98
Franklin, Benjamin, 113

Freedom of Information Act
    (FOIA), 54
Functions: ancillary, 26; core, 26

*General Requirements for a Presi-
    dential Library Building*, 25
Geselbrecht, Raymond, xv, xvi, xvii
    n.1
Graf, Leroy P., 125
Grant papers, 123, 125

Haldeman, H. R., 89
Harding, Florence K., 121
Harding, Warren G., 113, 121–23
Harding home, 123
Harding Memorial Association, 121
Harding papers, 121–23
Harrison, Benjamin, 4
Harrison, William H., 3
Hayes, Lucy Webb, 116
Hayes, Rutherford B., 113, 115–17
Hayes, Webb C., 115
Hayes Library, 115–17; William
    Dean Howells Collection, 116
Hayes Presidential Center, 115;
    The Statesman, 117
Henley, Clarence E., 36
Hirshon, Arnold D., 105
Holdings: collateral, 46; core, 46;
    kinds of, 41–42, 43. *See also un-
    der individual libraries*
Hoover, Herbert, National Histori-
    cal Site, 67
Hoover, Lou Henry, 68
Hoover Presidential Library, 67–70
Hopkins, William J., 32

Instructions to users, 51–55
Integral file segments, 8

Jackson papers, 123, 124
Jefferson papers, 123, 124
Johnson, Andrew, papers, 123, 125
Johnson, Lady Bird, 87
Johnson, Lyndon Baines, School of
    Public Affairs, 82
Johnson Presidential Library, 82–
    88

Joint Resolution of July 18, 1939, 5, 58
Jones, H. G., 58

Kennedy Presidential Library, 75–82; museum services, 80–81; Ernest Hemingway Collection, 77, 80
Kennedy, Robert F., 76
Kline, Ray, 22
Koucky, Judith A., 25

Library of Congress, 2, 6, 100, 111–14, 126 n.7
Library director, appointment of, 14–15
Lincoln, Abraham, 4
Link, Arthur S., 125
Loving, Benson, 116

Madison papers, 123–24
Maintenance, annual expenditures from 1955 to date, 19–21
Mandatory Declassification Review, 53
Mandatory endowments. See Endowments, mandatory
Marshall, John, 2
Massachusetts Historical Society, 117
Materials, disposal of, 14
Matthews, William F., 32
Michigan, University of, 93
Moser, Harold D., 124
Museum of the Presidents, explore demands for, 28

Nash, Thomas, 116
National Archives, 34–35, 89, 124, 125
National Historical Publications commission, 119, 122, 123
National Study Commission on Records and Documents of Federal Officials, 6–7, 10
Nixon, Richard, 6

Nixon Presidential Materials Project, 88–92
Nixon-Sampson agreement, 6–7

Office of Presidential Papers and Archives, 89
Ohio Historical Society, 121
O'Neill, James E., 37, 39 n.18, 97

Papers, 3–4, 123; eras in history of (Geselbrecht), xv, xvi, xvii n.1; immediate disclosure, chilling effect of, 11; private property, 1–2; public property, 11; Washington to Coolidge, 1–5, 105–15
Pennsylvania, Historical Society of, 120
Plavchan, Ronald J., 89
Polk, James K., 3, 123, 124, 125
Polk papers, 123, 124, 125
Preliminary inventories, 52
Presidential Libraries Act of 1955, 5, 63, 105; cost estimate, original, 18
Presidential Libraries Act of 1986, 15, 21, 27–28, 129; mandatory endowments under, 27–28
Presidential Recordings and Materials Preservation Act, 6–9, 10, 88; Title I, implemented by regulations, 7–9
Presidential Records Act, 11–14, 26
Prologue: Journal of the National Archives, 72

Reed, David J., 36
Registers, Library of Congress, used by, 52
Relyea, Harold C., 106
Research applications, 51–52
Research room procedures, 52
Restrictions, 8, 53–54
Ribicoff, Abraham, 8
Roosevelt, Franklin D. Library, Inc., 58
Roosevelt Presidential Library, 1–2, 57–63
Rutland, Robert A., 124

Sampson, Arthur F., 6
Sherman, John, 116
Sherman, William T., 116
Simon, John Y., 125
Smith, Thomas A., 115, 126 n.10
Sparks, Jared, 2
Staffing patterns, 49–50
State Department, papers gathered by, 2
Supporting organizations, 50–51, 139–45

Taft, William Howard, 4–5
Taylor, Willie Day, 84
Taylor, Zachary, 3
Title to buildings, 21
Truman, Harry S, Library Institute, 66–67
Truman Presidential Library, 63–67
Twohig, Dorothy, 124
Tyler, John, 3

Use, 42–46, 47–48
Users, instructions to, 51–55

Vice-presidential records, 15
Visitors, library. See Use

Walker, Celeste, 117, 118
Warner, Robert M., 22, 24, 97
Washington, Bushrod, 2
Washington, Corbin, sale of papers by, 2
Washington, George, 2, 3, 123, 124
Washington papers, 123, 124
Weeding, 36–37
White House Central Files, 32
White House liaison with National Archives, 34–35, 89
Whitman, Ann, 71
Wilson papers, 123, 125
Withdrawn materials, 52–53
Wood, Robert, 67
Woods, Rose Mary, 89

About the Author

FRITZ VEIT, Director of Libraries Emeritus, Chicago State University, is the author of *The Community College Library* (Greenwood Press, 1975) and articles in *College and Research Libraries, Library Trends,* and other journals, as well as a chapter in *Internationalizing Library and Information Science Education* (Greenwood Press, 1987).

About the Author